AF616774

THE

BRUNSWICK ACCESSION

THE

BRUNSWICK ACCESSION

BY

PERCY M. THORNTON

KENNIKAT PRESS
Port Washington, N. Y./London

THE BRUNSWICK ACCESSION

First published in 1887
Reissued in 1971 by Kennikat Press
Library of Congress Catalog Card No: 75-118506
ISBN 0-8046-1254-4

Manufactured by Taylor Publishing Company Dallas, Texas

PREFACE.

In dedicating this book to my friends E. Maunde Thompson and Edward Scott, of the Manuscript Department of the British Museum, I wish to recognise their kindness in drawing attention to the unedited Hanover Papers, owing to which I was induced to undertake my present task. It has been my object, by giving a succinct account of Her Majesty's family, and of the accession thereof to the British throne, to fill an obvious gap in our historical literature; while the time of publication seems opportune, falling, as it does, a few weeks before the Queen completes fifty years of her reign. But the work was originally designed, without reference to any such coincidence, as the result of historical research entered on for the sake of the subject itself and the interesting speculations necessarily suggested by the perplexing possibilities which hung in the air during the last years of Queen Anne's reign. There is no pretence here to have set aside the general conclusions of writers such as Mr. W. H. Lecky, Professor A. W. Ward, the late Rev. J. Green, or the late Lord Stanhope, but rather to have confirmed their conclusions; although the Record Office papers exonerate Lord Bolingbroke from the charge of carelessness in striving to defend the ports and harbours when, as Secretary of State, he was responsible for their maintenance in proper strength.

My justification for devoting so much space to the period 1702–1714 is that all through Queen Anne's reign extreme uncertainty as to the Succession prevailed, and the estimates of the chances of the rival claimants were various and fluctuating. Even among the rank and file of the Whigs and of the Protestant section of the Tories, there was, before 1710, little enthusiasm for the Hanoverians on the one side, or the Stuarts on the other, so that the Court influence was sufficient to turn the balance of public opinion. But professional statesmen could not tell from day to day whether that influence would veer right round or keep true to the star of Brunswick. It was difficult to understand that the Queen would remain steadfast in sacrificing her sisterly feelings to the interests of Protestantism, or that her brother would keep staunch to his faith at the peril of a crown; so that the above-named statesmen endeavoured to provide for their personal security in any event by paying furtive court both to Hanover and St. Germain. Thus assurances of loyalty to James Edward need not be held to imply the slightest intention to give him active support so long as the Queen continued to be in the same mind or James Edward in the same communion. These general considerations give weight to my contention that Lord Bolingbroke laboured as Secretary of State for two main objects, namely, loyal service to Queen Anne, and the elevation of the Tory party.

The affair of the writ for the Electoral Prince naturally raised the hopes of the Jacobites, but their restlessness only served to excite the apprehensions and determination of the Whigs, who were roused into something like enthusiasm by the Schism Bill—a measure which could hardly have been promoted by Oxford and Bolingbroke to bolster up their own failing power in Parliament if they had given one serious thought to the interests of the Stuart branch. They, and all well-informed statesmen, must have known that only the Queen's active advocacy could give her brother a reasonable chance of the throne so long as he remained a Papist. Thus Her Majesty's demise resolved the doubts of all moderate politicians in favour of the Guelphs, and so the Council, which naturally took the place of the Court at this juncture, accurately represented the general feeling of the nation when they at once proclaimed George the First as King. The outward expression of the fact that all uncertainty was at an end was the appearance of the Dukes of Somerset and Argyll in the Council-chamber. As matters turned out, the fears that the Jacobites would give trouble proved to be groundless, and at this distance of time seem almost foolish; for men who had long been clinging to a double hope of their ends being attained by constitutional means, could hardly be expected, when dismayed by the sudden extinction of those hopes, to be ready for an armed rising at a few hours' notice.

I have copied or mentioned several interesting papers omitted by Macpherson. The most striking statement amongst the unpublished Hanover Papers is that communicated by Sir William Dawes, Archbishop of York, containing an account of Queen Anne's voluntary denial of any intention to alter the Succession in 1714, and the document is therefore given at length. Nor is it of much less interest in reference to the Succession to know that that devoted Jacobite, James, second Duke of Ormond, wrote several letters expressing devotion to the Electoral Court at Hanover, during 1714; or that three years later (1717) Prince Eugene made similar professions to the exiled Prince James Edward at Avignon, when the great Imperialist general was there campaigning against the Turks.

Again, the mission of Lord Clarendon to Hanover, which is minutely described in the Hanover Papers, has been brought prominently into this narrative, and I have adduced evidence not hitherto made public in support of the opinion of recent writers that Bolingbroke desired to place the Tory party in power, rather than to alter the Succession, and bring in a Catholic King.

The fact that the great Duke of Marlborough's

earlier letters to the Court of St. Germain fell into Lord Oxford's hands has not hitherto been acknowledged by historians, although Lord Stanhope shows that he suspected as much when commenting on the abandonment of the prosecution directed in 1717 against Queen Anne's last Lord Treasurer.

The sketch which I have endeavoured to draw in the light of the Hanover Papers gives a very different idea of George the First to that hitherto current. Few are aware that the campaign of Blenheim was conceived in Council with the Elector.

The descriptions of the various alarms of invasion, as well as of threatened internal commotions which were extant in England during 1713–14, are very curious, and contain several statements never before published. These occur in the more recent series of papers at the Record Office, marked *Anne, Domestic*, and are, for the most part, contained in the chapter on Bolingbroke's designs, chap. ix.

With regard to the frequent quotations from Macpherson, his excerpts from the Hanover Papers being generally identical with the originals, it is reasonable to grant the credence never directly refused to this author, when he translates from cipher the Stuart papers which the President of the Scotch College at Paris allowed him to copy in 1770. Lord Caryll's letters are especially worthy of remark, because that nobleman was sent to Rome as the representative of James the Second, and remained in the Jacobite counsels to his death.

The same may be said of Lord Middleton, James Edward Stuart's political adviser, and various other correspondents, copies of whose communications Macpherson obtained. At the same time it is wise to observe great care in accepting the latter writer's deductions from these letters and memoranda; because, born at Kingussie, in the centre of the Highlands, Macpherson was a fervent Jacobite, and his writings bear the impress of such opinions. Macpherson will be also remembered for his controversy with Dr. Johnson regarding Ossian, whose poems the former claimed to have translated.

More than a general historical outline it has been found impossible to give, as a period of at least 250 years had to be traversed, not to mention the mediæval memories awakened by the early Guelphic records dealt with in the first two chapters.

As to 1688, and the deliverance effected by William the Third, the most remarkable piece of history brought prominently forward in this book is Dalrymple's exposure of the intrigue with Rome in 1688, whereby the Dutch diplomatists induced the Papal Court to advance a sum of money to enable William the Third to invade England and dethrone James the Second.

Apart from the presence of such hitherto unpublished matter as has been alluded to, it will, I hope, be found that much unfamiliar information has been collected from printed authorities and set forth in a convenient form.

The genealogical table is intended to present in a general view the most interesting steps in the pedigree which is traced in the following pages. I regret that I have been unable to find the name of the Emperor Lothair's only daughter, the wife of Henry the Proud. Cunigunda, as the heiress of the senior branch of the Guelphs, has to appear on the left of her husband, Azo the Second, Marquis d'Este.

PERCY M. THORNTON.

BATTERSEA RISE,
April, 1887.

CONTENTS.

CHAPTER IX.

CHAPTER X.

CHAPTER XI.

CHAPTER XII.

CHAPTER XIII.

ERRATA.

Page 244, 5th line of Appendix, *for* "1878" *read* "1868."

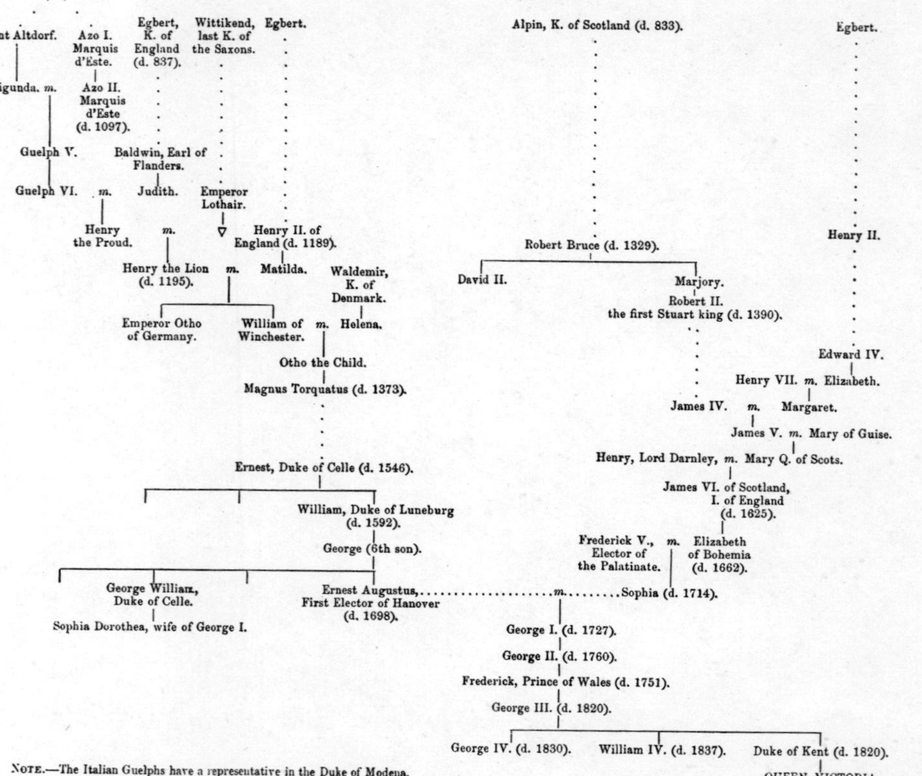

NOTE.—The Italian Guelphs have a representative in the Duke of Modena.

THE

BRUNSWICK ACCESSION.

CHAPTER I.

THE EARLY GUELPHS.

A.D. 450–1514.

THE researches of the philosopher and antiquarian Leibniz among the archives of Modena, in which he utilised the investigations of his contemporary Muratori, have made it possible to supplement and correct the current ideas about the origin and alliances of the House of Guelph, as to which much misconception seems still to prevail in Great Britain, though Leibniz made his discoveries public 1707–1717. But before this, the subjects of the Brunswick princes who lived in the sixteenth and seventeenth centuries could not fully appreciate the high antiquity which their family could claim. When, therefore, by the union of Ernest Augustus of Hanover with the Electress Sophia, what Leibniz subsequently proved to be the purest Teutonic blood of Europe was mingled with that of ancient Scottish kings, the result was a pedigree of unsurpassed splendour and antiquity.

Descended from Guelph, or Wlph, Prince of the Scyrri, one of the nations that fought under the banners of Attila the Hun, the Royal House of England likewise unites in its illustrious lineage the blood of the Saxon Egbert, King of England, who died A.D. 837, with that of his contemporary, the Celtic Alpin, King of Scotland.*

As regards the Guelphs, it is worthy of note that in a direct line from the above-mentioned Prince Guelph, or Wlph, were derived the two Marquesses of Este, successively known in German and Italian story as the first and second of that name. It is, therefore, an error to impute an Italian *origin* to our Royal house, whose earliest ancestors, so far as they have been traced, had their home in Bavaria.†

Azo, the second Marquess of Este in Italy (born A.D. 995, died 1097), the head of the Italian (junior) branch of Guelphs, married Cunigunda, the sole heiress of the German Guelphs of Altdorf, thus uniting in his family the blood, wealth, and power of both branches of the old Guelphs, and becoming the common father of the later German and Italian princes of the name of Guelph. No wonder, then, that he was elected by the Emperor, Henry the Third, as his representative in Italy. If the chroni-

* Sir Andrew Halliday's 'House of Guelph,' p. 203.

† Ibid., Introduction, p. 10.

clers of this period do not err, Azo d'Este the Second must have lived 102 years,* and he certainly possessed full command of his faculties late in that long life.

Cunigunda, the first wife of Azo the Second, bore him one son *Guelph*, who was known in German history as Guelph the Sixth. He succeeded to his mother's titles and vast estates on her death, A.D. 1055, and to those of his father, A.D. 1097. He had a high spirit, and loved the tented field; and Henry the Fourth invested him with the Duchy of Bavaria, A.D. 1071—a title first assumed one hundred and seventy years before (A.D. 900) by his almost mythological ancestor, Henry of the Golden Chariot. Guelph the Sixth married twice; first with a Bavarian princess, from whom he separated, notwithstanding that he retained her duchy, which then extended to the confines of Hungary; and secondly with Judith, daughter of Baldwin, Earl of Flanders. After a wandering soldier-life spent in espousing the cause of the Church, and consequently more often than not at variance with the Emperor, he made a disastrous crusade to the Holy Land, where he lost his army, and died on his return at Paphos, in the island of Cyprus, A.D. 1101. By the above-named Judith he left two sons, Guelph the Seventh, and Henry the Black, who successively ruled the Bavarian States.

Guelph the Seventh enjoyed great popularity both

* Sir Andrew Halliday's 'House of Guelph,' pp. 25, 26.

in Germany and at Rome, and was, therefore, frequently enabled to act as mediator between Pope and Emperor.

His brother, Henry the Black, Duke of Bavaria, succeeded him in the year 1125, and to this prince's influence the election of Lothair as Emperor of Germany was mainly due. Henry reigned, however, only six years, which, nevertheless, proved an important period, because great accessions of territory then accrued to the House of Guelph, as Henry took to wife Wilfilda, daughter and heiress of Magnus, the last of the Dukes of the Billung race, who then exercised sovereignty as Dukes of Saxony in the districts adjacent to the Hartz Mountains as well as over those near the rivers Weser and Leine.

Henry the Black and Wilfilda, the Princess of Billung, had three sons: Conrad, a monk, who died a year before his father, in 1126; Henry the Proud, Duke of Bavaria and Saxony; and Guelph the Eighth, Duke of Spoleto and Tuscany.

Henry the Proud having espoused a daughter of the Emperor Lothair the Second, not only acquired the remaining States of Saxony, but also became sovereign of Brunswick. Henceforth, by reason of his wife's lineal descent from Wittikend, the last Saxon King, he adopted the crest of a *white horse*, which device remains the family crest to this day. He was a loyal supporter of the Emperor Lothair the Second, when the banner of insurrection was raised by Frederick of Suabia, the defeated candidate for the Imperial purple. Henry reduced the cities of Ulm and Spires, and forced the pretenders to the throne to resign their claims, so that Lothair became undisputed monarch of Germany.

Verily, Henry the Proud may be described as a mighty Teuton, but after the Emperor Lothair the Second died, in 1137, it was not destined, as had been hoped and believed, that he should reap the reward of his former fidelity, and fill the coveted throne.

A combination comprising both ecclesiastical and secular princes, who were jealous of his power and enraged at his unbending demeanour, being formed against him, the election fell on Conrad, elder of the Ghibelline brothers, who resolved to detract from the defeated candidate's territorial sway by wrenching Saxony from his grasp.* To this, proud by nature as by name, Henry demurred, but in a diet where his enemies appeared in a majority, he was stripped of his inheritance, declared to be a rebel, and placed under the ban of the Empire.

Escaping, however, with but four followers from the banks of the Danube to those of the Elbe and Weser, Henry the Proud appealed not in vain to the States of Brunswick and Luneburg, who found an army to which flocked many Guelphic vassals of Suabia and Bavaria, anxious to strike for the rights of the man they believed to be their legal sovereign. Despite that the Emperor Conrad advanced to meet this formidable attack, the two parties never came to

* Sir A. Halliday's 'History of the House of Guelph,' pp. 36–7.

blows, and Henry the Proud died in camp, A.D. 1139,* leaving an only son, Henry, ten years of age, who is perhaps the most prominent of all Brunswick heroes under his well-known title, Henry the Lion. This child was destined to regain his father's territories, and to be remembered as the most chivalrous and refined sovereign of the time. He saved Brunswick from an incursion planned by the Emperor in 1147, and such was the respect engendered by his courage and ability, that when Frederick Barbarossa donned the Imperial purple in 1152, the value of the young Henry's alliance was apparent, and the Guelphic loyalty to the Empire became notorious in his person, while his striking capacity and dauntless spirit soon led men to respect his statesmanship, and fear his sword.

In the year 1157, Henry the Lion having gained back Bavaria, stood at the apex of his power, which extended from the Baltic to the Mediterranean. We are unable here to trace the causes of the decline of this prosperity, or to describe the romantic scenes of battle and chivalry through which he passed, but must rest content with telling how the Princess of England, Matilda, daughter of Henry the Second, became his bride in 1168, and how Brunswick, the place of residence mostly frequented by the Lion, was beautified and adorned by the Cathedral of St. Blase,† which he

* It was in the course of this campaign that the famous war cries, Guelph and Ghibelline, were first used, and became for 130 years familiar terms wherewith to describe the Ecclesiastical and Imperial factions in Italy.

† Dedicated to St. Blasius, the Apostle of Brunswick.

filled with relics collected during the second crusade. Moreover, it is interesting to remember how he gained Lubeck and made it a free port, and rendered Brunswick and her people famous in the world. Like his father, Henry the Proud, he was destined to quarrel with the holder of the Imperial Crown, and like him fell under the ban, becoming a wanderer over Europe, during which period of depression in his fortunes he was welcomed at Winchester by his father-in-law, Henry the Second, and stayed some time in England.

Frederick Barbarossa was latterly induced to adopt an attitude of such active hostility towards the Guelphs, that Henry returned home to defend his dominions, and it was only after a final campaign against the next Emperor, Henry the Sixth, carried on with English aid, King Richard the First furnishing troops, that Henry the Lion saved his beloved Brunswick from capture. It was, moreover, just previous to this siege in 1192, that this prince built Luneburg, the present capital of the duchy of that name.

When in the year 1192 Richard Cœur de Lion was returning from the Holy Land, the Duke of Austria, as is well known, seized his person. Henry the Sixth, Emperor of Germany, concurred in his detention, but two sons of the Lion, Otho and William of Brunswick, came forward, together with other German princes, and offered themselves as hostages for the ransom demanded by the Austrian

Duke, while Henry the Lion helped to negotiate the treaty for Richard's liberation, and stood security for the remainder of the money required.

Richard, on his part, did not leave Germany until he had gained forgiveness for Henry the Lion from the Emperor, and obtained restitution of some of his provinces, so that this remarkable ancestor of Queen Victoria died, in 1195, a power in the North of Germany.

Truly this incident, so creditable to the Guelphs, stands in history as an earnest of the happy union to be again cemented between England and Brunswick, when the cause of liberty was at stake amongst us.

By the Princess Matilda of England, Henry the Lion had three sons and two daughters, and with the exception of one of the latter who died young, they all became prominent figures in the chronicles of their times. The third and youngest of these sons was Queen Victoria's ancestor. He was born in England, and is known as William of Winchester. He married Helen, daughter of Waldemir, King of Denmark. The second son, Otho, received the highest honour within reach of any layman in the year 1198, when the Pope confirmed the election of a Guelph to the Imperial dignity.

But this supreme elevation was accomplished amidst a civil war which ravaged Germany; Philip of Suabia, son of the late Emperor, Henry the Sixth, endeavouring to assert his claims by force of arms. The truth seems to have been that there was a double election by different portions of the Empire. Philip, at first, gained ground, notwithstanding the Papal opposition, but was suddenly assassinated by Otho of Wittelsbach—Count Palatine—when the Suabian cause was at its brightest.*

Still, for a time, Otho the Fourth of Guelph was undisputedly wearer of the Imperial Crown, and, according to Sir Andrew Halliday's 'Annals of the House of Hanover' (Book V., p. 355), it was the English influence that secured the throne for Otho after Philip's death.

The Pontiff, however, upon the refusal of the Emperor to abandon his rights over Italy, went over to his enemies. Internecine conflicts continued until 1214, when a Papal excommunication, following upon the ill success of his arms, caused Otho to resign. He lived in retirement at Brunswick until 1218. As he had not increased his father's—Henry the Lion's—possessions, the practical result of the efforts of Henry the Proud and his son Henry the Lion, to make conquests north of the Elbe, was this, that a coalition of neighbouring states was formed, which succeeded in reducing the Brunswick power within the limits of the territories known geographically by the name of Hanover.†

Henceforth the Guelphs appear as ordinary German

* Hallam's 'Middle Ages.' Seventh Ed., 1838, vol. ii. p. 104.

† Owing much to Sir A. Halliday's 'House of Guelph,' the author desires likewise to acknowledge his indebtedness for some facts in the above sketch to an article in the *Edinburgh Gazetteer* of 1822, p. 211. The statements therein bear the closest test which research can bring.

princes, and the terms Brunswick, Luneburg, Wolfenbüttel, Grubenhagen, alternate one with another, the Dukes who ruled over those territories being frequently forced to defend the homesteads of their people.

The town of Brunswick especially suffered from attack, and the spirit engendered by Henry the Lion, who shares the distinction of tutelar saint in the locality with St. Blase, was again and again invoked to save the coveted city from destruction. Albert the Great, who died in 1279, and Magnus the Pious, who died in 1369, were amongst the more famous Dukes of Brunswick, while the story of Magnus Torquatus the Chain-bearer, Duke of Brunswick and Luneburg, who died in 1373, is of itself a romance, for the recital of which we would fain find space. But the exigencies of our subject bid us push on, mentioning *en passant* that Duke Bernhard invaded Brandenburg in 1389, taking its fortresses and devastating the country, but was in turn punished by the Bishop of Osnaburg, who found allies to revenge his wrongs,* and also, that Frederick, Duke of Brunswick, when elected King of the Romans, set out for Frankfort to receive the Imperial crown, and was foully murdered on his journey in the year 1400.

William the Victorious, who died A.D. 1503 at the age of 90, merits mention, and so does Henry of Brunswick-Wolfenbüttel, yclept the Bad (killed in

* Sir A. Halliday's 'House of Guelph,' p. 87.

1514)—a title always affixed to his name, for no apparent reason, as he was a capable general. Probably the explanation lies in the fact that he was the only Duke of Brunswick who drew sword against the citizens of his capital—namely, when they had joined the Hanseatic League, and declared themselves a free city. Henry the Bad, by negotiation, received nominal submission, but the people, probably, never forgave him.

Thus is the history of this noble family traced from the mists of antiquity, and through the Middle Ages, when, feudality becoming the general law of Europe, men considered it an honour to hold of the Empire.

We have, however, approached a time when unexpected elements of strife appeared in Germany, Luther's assertion of religious dependence on Bible truth, rather than on ecclesiastical exposition thereof, having agitated the world, and split mankind into two camps. In the territories of Brunswick-Luneburg, the new ideas were not accepted without protest, nor could it so be, when the Emperor of Germany frowned on opinions which claimed for man a right to think for himself, only waiting for a good opportunity to become actively hostile, by joining hands with the spiritual power at Rome for the purpose of stamping out the startling opinions which Luther proclaimed in 1517.

But on the whole the balance of opinion amongst the Brunswickers seems to have been adverse to Rome at this period. If it be desired to realise in some degree the personalities of the illustrious rulers and warriors of old Brunswick, let the reader betake himself in imagination to Henry the Lion's Cathedral of St. Blase, where many of their mortal remains are interred. Standing on the site of a former ecclesiastical edifice, viz., the church of St. Peter and St. Paul, this fine building was finished in 1194, the first prince of quality whose tomb is preserved being Eckbert the Second, Margrave of Brunswick, who died during the raising of the holy fane wherein his ashes lie. The Emperor Henry the Fourth not being able to conquer Eckbert in open war, paid for his assassination, the Abbess Adelheid of Quedlingburg, the Emperor's sister, being concerned in the murder.

He was originally buried in St. Syriacin church, which he had founded; but when this edifice was pulled down in the siege of 1542, Eckbert's stone coffin was brought to St. Blase's and opened, when the skull was seen to be pierced mortally, the appearance of the injury in question bearing out the story that Eckbert had been killed by a hatchet.

The student of 12th-century Teutonic lore will feel the deepest interest in the tomb of the Lion, who is said to have died on a Sunday, August 6th, 1195, and was buried with his wife, Matilda of England, Henry the Second's daughter, tradition telling us that at the time of the Lion's funeral two other coffins were in the vault, that of Matilda, and Otho, a son who died young.

An elevated monument surmounts this tomb, on the top of which are the figures of Henry and his wife, the founder of the Cathedral, bearing a small model of the building in his right hand.

In what is called the old vault of St. Blase are interred thirteen Brunswickian princes and princesses, including Otho the Fourth, the Emperor, Beatrix, the Empress, Albert the Great, Magnus Torquatus, Frederick, Emperor elect, but who never wore the purple, as he was assassinated on his way to Frankfort.

This tomb, being opened mysteriously in the year 1606 by what was said to have been an earthquake, has since been covered by a brass plate, inscribed with some biographical facts, which rests upon an otherwise bald flat stone in the nave before the choir. Most of the other monuments in the Cathedral have reference to later periods, such as a study of our narrative may invest with an interest with which they can scarcely inspire the uninstructed observer, as the evidences of nobility are hidden from the public eye.*

But nevertheless the contemplation of those ancient aisles brings home to the visitor how long a line of princely ancestors the Guelphs can claim, while connecting this Walhalla of the race with the memory of Henry the Lion, greatest Guelph of the Middle Ages. But we must bid adieu to mediæval memories, and seek those connected with more modern story.

* For these later details I am indebted to Sir A. Halliday's 'House of Guelph,' pp. 265–270.

CHAPTER II.

THE PROTESTANT BRANCH OF ENGLAND'S ROYAL HOUSE.

A.D. 1517–1701.

ERNEST, Duke of Celle,* surnamed the Confessor, and born in 1497, appropriately links together the traditions of Guelph d'Este and Henry the Lion with those of modern times, and he likewise occupies a leading position amongst those sovereigns and statesmen mentioned in the present chapter.

This Ernest of Brunswick, Duke of Celle, was ancestor to the present Royal Family of England, and may be selected as a representative of those peculiar qualities which induced the English nation to choose their dynasty from the Brunswick-Luneburg line.

One of the princes who entered into the league of Protestant States against the all-powerful Charles the Fifth, Ernest had so much to do with forwarding Reformation principles in Germany that his name appropriately heads this page, and when we add that as a youth he studied under Luther at Wittenberg, was a zealous supporter of the great

* Thus modern authorities spell the familiar "Zell."

religious reformer, being taken prisoner with the Elector of Saxony, when Charles the Fifth revenged himself upon the Protestants at the battle of Muhlburg in 1547, our readers will recognise his title to prominence. He married a daughter of the Duke of Mecklenburg. Duke Ernest's power, wealth, and honours, devolved on his third son, William, who became Duke of Luneburg, and allied himself with the House of Denmark; his wife Dorothea, daughter of Christian the Third of that kingdom, bearing him no less than seven sons and eight daughters,* whose careers we are precluded from describing exhaustively.

It is, however, interesting to know that Duke William's eldest son Otho wished to marry Mary Tudor of England, and offered her brother, Edward the Sixth, 10,000 men to act against France at the same time that he made his matrimonial proposal. The Lady Mary had then been promised to the Infant of Portugal, while England and France concluded peace; but the incident is curious, as showing how the course of history might have been altered had Queen Mary been given in marriage to a Protestant Brunswick instead of to Philip the Second, that absentee husband whose cruelties in Spain, perpetrated in the cause of religion, stamp him as a monarch far behind his times.

Not so the gallant Brunswickers, who again and

* 'Some Account of the House of Brunswick-Luneburg,' Macpherson's 'Original Papers,' vol. i. p. 612.

again espoused the cause of oppressed people; when, for instance, by Duke Christian, son of William, Duke of Luneburg, succour was given to the unfortunate Frederick, King of Bohemia, and his beautiful spouse, the English Princess Elizabeth, whose romantic adventures will be treated in another chapter.

This notable Duke Christian died of a fever at Wolfenbüttel, in 1626. His two brothers, Augustus and Frederick, proved themselves worthy of their fraternity by striking for the Protestant cause throughout the various wars of the high-souled Gustavus Adolphus,* and were concerned in all the transactions of Germany early in the 17th century. Duke William's above-mentioned seven sons having all except George died and left no male issue, the Brunswick duchies fell to the four sons of the said George, whose wife was a Princess of Hesse-Darmstadt.

The *first*, Christian Lewis, took to his share the Duchies of Celle and Luneburg, and died without issue in 1665; his *second* brother, George William, inheriting his honours and possessions.

This Duke, whose personal history is bound up with that of the English Royal Family, married Eleanor, a daughter of a French Marquess of Poitou, Olbrenze by name, and the child of that alliance, Sophia Dorothea, was wife to her cousin, the second Elector of Hanover, George the First of England.

The *third* brother of this generation was John

* 'Some Account of the House of Brunswick-Luneburg,' Macpherson's 'Original Papers,' vol. i. p. 613.

Frederick, Duke of Hanover, a renegade from the Brunswick principles, who allied himself with Louis the Fourteenth, and endeavoured to influence other members of his family. John Frederick died on the way to Rome, in 1680, remaining a fervent Catholic to the last; while the Fates smiled brightly on the marriage of the *fourth* brother, Ernest Augustus (who became Elector of Hanover),* with the Princess Sophia, daughter of Frederick, Elector Palatine, and King of Bohemia.

The life of Ernest Augustus, first Elector of Hanover, is probably more interesting to a student of the Brunswick succession than that of any other potentate of Guelph origin. In the first place, he allied himself with the Stuarts by espousing James the First's granddaughter, and was not only advanced by the Emperor Leopold to the honourable position of Elector, a ninth vote being thenceforth appended to the rulership of Hanover, at William the Third's request, as a reward to Ernest Augustus for his fidelity to the anti-French cause; but he likewise introduced primogeniture into that branch of the Brunswick-Luneburg family which he represented, and he ultimately inherited George William Duke of Celle's honours and possessions.

* In 1692 the Emperor Leopold, at the instigation of William the Third, King of England, created a ninth Electorate, in the person of Duke Ernest, as a reward for his fidelity to the Protestant cause. The duty of an Elector of the Holy Roman Empire was under ordinary circumstances at this period little more than nominal, because the head of the Hapsburg family was by general consent chosen to the position. The House of Austria ruled supreme in Germany at this period.

Hitherto the territories of the Brunswick-Luneburg family had been irregularly assigned to the various children of the princes who ruled in Celle and Hanover, but Duke Ernest Augustus made an eldest son of George Lewis, and so laid the foundation of that Hanoverian Principality which played so important a part in the eighteenth century, blossoming into a kingdom after the Napoleonic wars.

But by this action a result peculiarly pertinent to the present subject was attained: George Lewis, acknowledged as the representative of a solidified Electorate, could offer an alliance not to be ignored when the balance of European power was threatened; and William the Third, with a true statesman's acumen perceiving this, persuaded the British Legislature to adopt the Brunswick-Luneburg family as successors to Queen Anne, provided that sovereign died without issue.

Hanover, although territorially speaking not an extensive dominion, was notoriously rich in natural resources,* and a large revenue pertained to its sovereigns, who ruled over a population estimated at about half a million only,† which yet maintained

* The mineral products of the Hartz mountains have contributed to render Hanover a well-to-do country. The first silver mines discovered in Europe were opened here in 968, while iron, copper, lead, zinc and sulphur have all been obtained from the soil. For the conveyance of merchandise the Elbe, Weser, Aller and Embs are favourably situated, while in Brunswick proper the wool and linen trades have flourished, and the spinning-wheel is said to have been invented there.

† Morris's 'Early Hanoverians,' p. 21.

a disproportionately large military force, amounting in Duke Ernest Augustus's time to 15,000 men.

The value of such an ally as the Elector of Hanover, during the wars of Louis the Fourteenth with the Empire, will be duly appraised when these circumstances are understood.

The children of Ernest Augustus and the Princess Sophia were as follows :—

(1) George Lewis, afterwards George the First of England—born in 1660 : died 1727.

(2) Frederick Augustus, born in 1661 : killed fighting against the Turks, in 1685.

(3) Maximilian, born in 1666 : died in 1726.

(4) Charles Philip, born in 1669 : slain in the Turkish war.

(5) Christian, born in 1671 : drowned in the Danube, 1703.

(6) Ernest Augustus, born in 1671 : died unmarried, 1728.

(7) Sophia Charlotta, born in 1668 :* married Frederick the First of Prussia, dying Queen of that kingdom in 1705.

Of George Lewis we have much to say hereafter. Frederick Augustus and Charles Philip commanded the contingent of 10,000 men, which the house of Brunswick-Luneburg sent to help the Emperor in his war with the Turks in 1684. These two gallant soldiers died in battle.

* Burke's 'Peerage,' p. 84.

Maximilian went to the Morea, as chief of an auxiliary force which his father allowed to serve the Venetian Republic. He entered upon duties there in 1686. After two creditable campaigns the Republic made him a General, and gave him a pension of 6000 ducats. Upon his return, Maximilian formed a party to support his assumed rights to the duchy of Celle; but after several adherents had been executed and he himself imprisoned, he renounced his pretensions, and, when war was declared after Louis the Fourteenth had acknowledged the Pretender in 1701 and put his grandson on the throne of Spain, entered the Imperial service.

Christian, like his brothers, Frederick Augustus and Charles Philip, died a soldier's death, but not by the sword, as he lost his life when attempting to swim over the Danube, in 1703.*

Ernest Augustus, the Princess Sophia's youngest son, Bishop of Osnaburg, accompanied George Lewis to England in 1714, and enjoyed the honours due to a prince of the blood, being created Duke of York, Albany, and Ulster. He never married, and, surviving all his brothers, died in 1728.

Truly it may be said of the Princess Sophia, that she was alike mother of princes and warriors; while her only daughter, Sophia, died as first Queen of Prussia in 1705, having married the Duke of Brandenburg who first attained to regal dignity.

* 'Some Account of the House of Brunswick,' Macpherson's 'Original Papers,' vol. i. p. 616.

We have narrated these details connected with the Electress Sophia's German relations, because the remarkable services of the race to freedom on the European Continent are sometimes forgotten; whilst the literature of this century is by no means sufficiently impressive in regard to the fact that the Brunswick-Luneburg family were chosen to succeed Queen Anne, because English society preferred government by those of kindred race to a Franco-Italian rule of Jesuit flavour.

It will be well, anyhow, that the reader of historical and domestic literature between 1701–14 should clear the mind of a good deal of cant, and should comprehend that through the veins of the British Royal Family courses the finest Stuart blood, while they boast also an ancestry of Teutonic origin, whose loves, woes, and deaths are as worthy the wizard pen of a Scott as are those of the exiled branch of the Stuarts, whose sufferings Sir Walter's genius has surrounded with an unfading glow of romance.

It is well known that old friendship with her Stuart cousins long rendered the Electress Sophia a hesitating claimant for the English throne, and that her doubts not only took the form of that famous so-called Jacobite letter to Stepney, the diplomatist,*

* "If I were thirty years younger, I should have a sufficiently good opinion of my birth and of my religion to believe that I should be appreciated in England. But as there is little probability of my surviving two people much younger, although more subject to ordinary dangers than myself, it is to be feared that at my death my sons would be regarded as

but that, despite her family indebtedness to the King of England, she had the courage to avow something akin to sorrow for James the Second's misfortunes.

"I believe (she wrote to William on his elevation to the throne) you cannot doubt of the part which I take in everything that contributes to your elevation and your glory; yet I lament King James, who honoured me with his friendship." *

The most she ever admitted was in conversation to Leibniz, "that the unfortunate James had brought about his own destruction;" and when made heiress to the throne, she silently accepted the position of the head of Protestantism in the Royal House of England, but acted so that she would not have had crude opinions to withdraw, or undue assumption of authority to resign, if another member of her family nearer to the main branch had been clothed in the purple by desire of the English people, whose temper as regards the succession was judged to be uncertain.†

---

strangers, the eldest of whom is much more accustomed to claim a high prerogative as sovereign than the poor Prince of Wales, who is too young to profit by the example of the King of France, and who would apparently be so glad to recover that which the King, his father, has so inconsiderately lost, that they would be able to do with him just what they wished.

"I am not so philosophical nor so thoughtless that you should think I do not like to hear a crown spoken of, and that I do not give due consideration to the weighty judgment you have given on this subject. It seems to me that in England there are so many parties that one can be sure of nothing. That does not prevent my being much obliged, &c., &c."—This is a translation from the original.

* 'Life of James II., by himself,' vol. ii. p. 362. Dalrymple ('Memoirs,' vol. iii. p. 232) asserts that the Electress Sophia was "no friend to William III."

† Students with time at command should consult the correspondence of the Electress at the British Museum; also her letters in the Hanover

The Electress, although of the Calvinist persuasion, took personally a tolerant view of those differing from her, believing, as she told Madame de Brinon, "in the goodness of God;" while she approved of the English liturgy, but reprobated Roman Catholicism as being contrary to Christianity.*

The influence of Leibniz seems to have helped to form her character, which stands as the very embodiment of the reformed opinions which were contained in the English Church settlement, even if her theological training led to adoption of the earlier views taught us by the Genevan exiles in 1559 rather than those superadded by Laud and incorporated after the Reformation in 1662. So far the theological side of the character of this excellent Princess. In her old age, surrounded by kinsmen of different ages, she, the great-granddaughter of Mary Queen of Scots, was destined to look upon her own great-grandson, Frederick Prince of Wales, who in turn was great-grandfather to Her Majesty Queen Victoria.

It is a remarkable fact, that if George the Second had died young, none of his five uncles leaving issue, the Crown of England must have devolved on the King of Prussia's heirs, and Frederick the Great would have reigned at St. James's as well as at Potsdam. The reason for this is not far to seek. The younger

---

collection there; while the remarkably exhaustive article of Professor A. W. Ward, 'English Historical Review,' vol. i. p. 470, should be carefully studied, as giving the substance of German opinion as well as English.

* Macpherson's 'Original Papers,' vol. ii. p. 500.

sons of the Electress Sophia, not having equal shares in the duchies and principalities of Hanover, led roving lives, and left no issue, while the future Elector's two children were George the Second of England, and Sophia Dorothea, named after her ill-fated mother, of whom anon. The younger princess of that name, who might in a certain contingency have been heir to the throne of England, became wife to Frederick William the First of Prussia, and mother of the Great Frederick.* It is indeed difficult to imagine the latter reading his royal speech to a British Legislature, nor is it possible to conceive Potsdam grenadiers located in London.

George the First of England has not had justice done to him by the various chroniclers who have taken up the pen to describe those events which led to his enthronement at Westminster Abbey. The earlier portion of his life was spent in continental embroilments, and his constant care had been the preservation of the dukedom committed to his charge. Nor had the endorsement of the Electress Sophia's claims by the English Parliament rendered his home task the easier. The jealousy of neighbouring princes was naturally accentuated, if not originally aroused, by the prospective alliance verging on absolute union with powerful Britain, so that the Elector of Hanover found employment for all available means and

* 'Biographie Universelle,' tome xv. p. 79. Eng. Cyclop., vol. ii. p. 1015. Art. "Frederick the Great."

energies in striving to keep his Electorate faithful to the Imperial cause.

Like his brothers, George the First had served early in the tented field. Born in the year of Charles the Second's Restoration, viz., 1660, the young Prince of Osnaburg was only fifteen when he served in the campaign of 1675 under his father, being present at the Battle of Consarbrück, and the Siege of Treves.

On the latter occasion Marshal Crequi was taken prisoner, after having suffered the first French defeat recorded for sixty years*—a disaster which may be described as an afterwave, following the great Turenne's death, which a chance shot on the Rhine occasioned but a few weeks before. This calamity to Louis the Fourteenth's army released a portion of the Imperialist forces, and rendered the above-mentioned victory possible.

Loving fighting better than learning,† the future English King hied him towards whatever portion of Europe seemed to offer hopes of active service, and in this manner he passed through Hungary, the Morea, Germany, and Flanders; these places being at different times the scenes of his military adventures.

In 1679, this son of the Elector Ernest Augustus and Sophia, granddaughter of James the First, had visited France, and endeavoured, in the character of

* Hume, vol. viii. p. 19.

† 'Memoirs of Sophia Dorothea,' 1845, vol. i. p. 77, also Macpherson's 'Original Papers,' vol. i. p. 617.

diplomatist, to improve the relations of his father with the French Monarchy; while he extended these political travels into England, and there paid his addresses fruitlessly to the Princess Anne, kissing her with Charles the Second's consent, although the Court scarcely gave him the welcome which a favoured suitor might expect.*

The influence of England was not then thrown into the scale of Imperial interest, because Charles the Second elected to live and die subservient to France, in order that his personal needs might receive that momentary satisfaction which alone can attend desires having root neither in morality nor patriotic impulse.

Hence, it is not difficult to understand why the young George Lewis, Electoral Prince of Hanover—for so he was named when his father succeeded to the Duchy—was not received with perfect cordiality by the English Court during his sojourn at the British metropolis in 1681.

A Lutheran prince, whose father had drawn the sword with success against Charles the Second's secret ally, Louis the Fourteenth, was not likely to find favour in the eyes of the English King, or of his fraternal counsellor, the Roman Catholic Duke of York, who afterwards prosecuted a similar policy of veiled dependence on the Bourbons, at a time when he desired to change or ignore the laws at home. But despite his advances not being received

* 'The Early Hanoverians,' by F. E. Morris, p. 17.

with acclaim by the Princess Anne,* or specially favoured by her royal relations, the Electoral Prince of Hanover received a notable welcome from the University of Oxford.

All accounts concur in allowing that the departure of the Electoral Prince from England was caused by receiving an imperative message from his father, the semi-episcopal Duke of Hanover, who had other matrimonial views for that son of high destiny.

A marriage of expediency had been negotiated for him by his father, and the beautiful Sophia Dorothea, daughter and heiress of the wealthy George William, Duke of Celle, who desired to unite the duchies of Celle and Luneburg, was induced to marry her cousin, which resolution she expressed in a letter to her intended mother-in-law, known in history as the Electress Sophia. This union, which secured unity and consequent wealth in the family of Brunswick, took place in November 1682, and the prospect of happiness seemed exceedingly bright for the young couple.

On the 30th of October, 1683, a son, George Augustus, afterwards George the Second of England, was born; and, despite much absence from home, the amenities of married life were observed by the young

* In the case of ordinary individuals outside royalty, love seldom follows immediately on first sight, and it cannot be shown that George Lewis underwent any remarkable experience when he left England in haste without renewing his suit, and therefore open to make that unfortunate alliance with his cousin—an alliance arranged for family purposes, which marred the lives of George the First and Sophia Dorothea.

people until just before the birth of the Princess Sophia Dorothea, in 1686; this child, named after her mother, being, as we have previously said, destined to be for ever famous as the Queen of Prussia, whose son was Frederick the Great. Then, alas! jealous intrigues at the Hanoverian Court having sown the seeds of dissension between George Lewis and Sophia Dorothea, the drawbacks of a wild soldier life, when a young and beautiful bride remained at home, became but too apparent; yet George Lewis was encouraged by his father in keen pursuit of that profession of arms which afforded scope for improving their joint political interests at a time when the unsettled state of English politics seemed to offer a prospect of accession to the British throne, because, as head of the Protestant branch of England's Royal House, the Princess Sophia's rights would descend to her son, George Lewis.

Hence followed military service on behalf of the Emperor Leopold during the campaign against the Turks in 1683; while three years later these wandering expeditions dedicated to Mars culminated, so far as the Empire was concerned, at the capture of Buda in 1686.

The Emperor rewarded these efforts of the Brunswick-Luneburg family on his behalf by making Ernest Augustus Elector of Hanover in the year 1692. The close of the Turkish war left the Electoral Prince, George Lewis, free to place his sword at the disposal of another well-wisher and willing benefactor.

William, Prince of Orange, was the grandson of Charles the First of England; but Holland was his home, and the honour of that country the main object of life-long solicitude openly professed by a statesman, whose warrior instincts were chastened by an ever-ready appeal to the dictates of the brain and mind rather than to those of the heart. He lives in history not only as a great sovereign, but also as a general of marked ability, skilled in affairs beyond any of the contemporary princes, and, above all, the possessor of an iron will, which, if it tenanted a weak body, yet ever prevailed in moments when, great events being in the balance, prompt resolve could alone determine the destiny of events.*

William, as husband of the Princess Mary, was in communication with the Protestants in England, and his cause on the Continent was bound up with the same religious opinions. Therefore it came to pass that George Lewis served willingly under the Prince of Orange in Holland, seeing much active service, and was consequently a frequent visitor at the Loo or the Hague. He was present at the battles of Steenkirk and Landen, and witnessed the siege of Namùr; on each of these occasions gaining

* The Marshal Duke of Berwick, son of James the Second of England and Arabella Churchill, first saw William the Third at Landen, and in wrapt admiration likened his countenance to an eagle's.

good opinions of his valour and capacity from the shrewd leader of the Protestant coalition.

During these long periods of absence the Princess Sophia Dorothea was far from happy, being exposed to the observation which prominence at her father-in-law's Court entailed. Duke Ernest Augustus, despite that he was Bishop of Osnaburg, had striven to vie with Louis the Fourteenth in splendour, so far as the minor capabilities of his State allowed, and the *morale* of the *entourage* was not one whit higher than that which obtained at Versailles, so that the low tone which prevailed rendered it the more obligatory on those having influence to regulate their lives by the strictest rule.

Now it happened that the temperament of the Princess Sophia Dorothea did not allow her to participate in the life of the Elector's Court, and yet stand aloof from the society of those whose own lives were moulded on no strict lines of right and wrong. Among such, in all charity be it said, truth demands that we should class Count Köningsmark. A man of the world, in the bad sense of the term, he had early in life paid his addresses to the engaging Sophia Dorothea; until, by reason of her elevation to the rank of Princess, his hopes of gaining her hand were relegated to what should have been under ordinary circumstances a sage oblivion.

Now the writer of this book has carefully examined the evidence which exists concerning this assumed intrigue between Köningsmark and the Princess

Sophia Dorothea; and having taken his evidence from a work derived from original documents, which is admittedly hostile to the Brunswick dynasty,* he yet unhesitatingly declares, that beyond an unwisdom not unlikely to be found when a young wife is left too much alone by her husband and devoid of good counsellors, there is no ground for charging infidelity against the wife of George the First of England.† On the other hand, with equal desire to adjust the scales of justice, let us record the fact that this unfortunate princess, for reasons which, considering the sacredness of the marriage vow and the peculiar delicacy of her own position, we must declare *totally inadequate*, refused to resume the position of wife in George Lewis's household.

By so doing she affixed a stigma on her husband's name, and indicated a hostile spirit which could not leave any hope that she would again act tenderly

* 'Memoirs of Sophia Dorothea,' London, Colburn, 1845, known to be by the late Dr. Doran.

† Ibid., vol. i. p. 246. The Princess testified solemnly to her innocence by partaking of the sacrament before the chief officers of the Courts of Celle and Hanover. Moreover, the Elector Ernest Augustus had himself declared her to be guiltless of the charge of infidelity. She was condemned for deserting her husband. A view identical with that supported by documentary evidence in the 'Memoirs of Sophia Dorothea' is expressed in Coxe's 'Walpole,' vol. i. p. 269. Sir R. Walpole and Queen Caroline maintained her innocence after hearing both sides.—Coxe's 'Walpole,' vol. i. p. 269.

The imputation cast on Sophia is there declared to have been adjudged false and unjust, while this reaction in opinion is shown to have taken place after the deaths of the first two Electors of Hanover, Ernest Augustus, and George the First of England.

It is, however, fair to state that Coxe had previously recorded the story current in Hanoverian Court circles, and that Thackeray, in his 'Four Georges,' edition 1861, p. 31, adopted a view antagonistic to Sophia Dorothea.

towards him or consider his political interests. And so the hard, policy-guided Hanoverian statesmen placed her in durance at the Castle of Ahlen, where, although she was allowed local freedom of action and a petty Court, composed of those who were by no means entirely her own choice, yet she suffered the agony of a separation from her children; while a perpetual cloud was very unwisely, as we think, thrown over her own and her soldier-husband's future lives. And indeed the story had been too tragic to escape unfriendly repetition where-ever the enemies of the Brunswick dynasty—and they were legion—met together to tell how, after an interview with the Princess Dorothea, Köningsmark had been set upon as he left the Palace, and, when defending himself, suffered a violent death.*

Now we are not prepared to enter into the controversy as to whether the mistakes of husband or wife were most flagrant during the course of this ill-assorted alliance; but, in justice to George Lewis, it must be stated that a full and legally-equipped court of law at Hanover, which never suggested that the Princess had been guilty of any fault but that of coldness and indifference to her husband, yet

* "When Admiral Cammock, an Irish Jacobite, escaped from the destruction of the Spanish fleet of which he had commanded a wing, off Messina in 1718, he addressed an appeal from Malta directed to Admiral Byng, the British Admiral, asking him to desert and join the Pretender's standard. In this document, to which further allusion will be made, he speaks slightingly of George I. as having confined his wife for over thirty years in Ahlen Castle, because she had been engaged in a criminal intrigue with Köningsmark."—See 'Hanover Papers, Miscellaneous.'

failed to induce her to re-enter the Electoral Prince's household, and that she gladly acquiesced for her part in the sentence pronounced by this same tribunal, which declared "the ties of matrimony to be entirely dissolved and annulled." *

It is, of course, possible to argue that a wise policy would have dictated a different course than that adopted by the Electoral advisers, when, jealously watching and guarding this fair prisoner, they prevented her own story from reaching the public ear in England. For, in the year 1694, as a glance at Macpherson's 'Original Papers' † will show, the restoration of James the Second to the throne of England was not an improbable event, while, as cadets of the Royal House, with a contingent, if remote, claim to succeed, the family of the Electress Sophia could ill afford to allow calumnies of a most terrible description to be spread all over England by the agents and friends of an unfortunate lady, who, whatever her wrongs—and they certainly did exist, to some extent—was animated by an uncompromising spirit towards her husband. His charges of disobedience and coldness were met by others on the lady's side, which, if true, proved that the bad example of Louis the Fourteenth and Augustus of Poland ‡ had been followed by a prince who learnt his morals in the

* 'Memoirs of Sophia Dorothea,' vol. i. p. 268.

† Vol. i. p. 472, and following pages.

‡ Augustus of Poland had a terribly dissolute Court.

rough military school then rampant in Europe, and who found no corrective to any loose habits which he might have contracted, when he visited his father Ernest Augustus's Court at Hanover. An "authorized version" of the actual facts of the case could not have done more harm to George Lewis than the sedulous dissemination of virulent accusations by his enemies, and their mysterious suggestions of still darker doings; while, by exposing the animus of his wife and her partisans, it might even have tended to clear the husband's reputation.

Be that as it may, the quarrel between husband and wife was a deeply-seated evil, and, thanks to evil counsellors, such as the Baroness Platen, who, rumour said, had intrigued to bring these troubles about, and also, as some whispered, compassed Köningsmark's death, never was healed.

During the year 1698, George Lewis succeeded his father in the newly created Electorate of Hanover, which had then been in existence six years, so that until this work draws to a close, we shall henceforth know him as the Elector of Hanover, while his son, afterwards George the Second, took the title of Electoral Prince, each male representative of the Brunswick-Luneburg family remaining but a subject, so far as English prospects of royalty were concerned, to the Electress Sophia, widow of Ernest Augustus, through whose Stuart blood the late Elector's children became heirs to the British throne.

These facts and dates have been given once more with such clearness as the matter demands, on the ground that, as Demosthenes has it, "repetition secures attention," and that their recital, it may be hoped, will enable the present narrative to flow clearly and shortly to its end.

In the royal vault at Hanover, under the choir of the chapel built by Duke John Frederick, rest the remains of several later celebrities belonging to the House of Brunswick-Luneburg. Amongst these are Duke John Frederick himself, Ernest Augustus, the first Elector, the Electress Sophia, and George the First. Duke John Frederick was the last person interred with the rites of the Roman Catholic religion in this Royal place of worship, and the monks performed the ceremony with great solemnity. The Duke died on his way to Italy in 1679.*

Several other members of the Brunswick-Luneburg race are buried at Herzberg, while various monuments of their kinsmen remain scattered over the Duchy of Hanover amidst the various mediæval towns with which that country is studded.

In another chapter we shall attempt to describe how the sovereign and statesmen of England had acted in regard to the Brunswick succession.

* Sir A. Halliday's 'House of Guelph,' p. 460.

CHAPTER III.

COUNSELS OF WINDSOR AND ST. STEPHENS.

A.D. 1612–1701.

TURNING to England, it becomes necessary to examine, first, the dynastic origin of the present Royal Family, as traced from its Stuart progenitors distinct from German sources, and, secondly, to tell how the historical aspect of the question was viewed by the statesmen who brought the Brunswick succession into train, and made it legally necessary for future parliaments and ministries to claim priority for those members of the Royal Family professing the Protestant faith, whenever a fresh crisis should arise.

James the First of England had three children by his wife, Anne of Denmark, viz :—

(1) *Henry*, the brave and high-spirited prince, whose premature death plunged England in woe during the year 1612, he being the hope of the Puritan party then gaining strength, so that it was said in a contemporary ballad :—

"Henry the 8 puld down Abbyes and cells,
But Henry the 9 will pul down Bishops and bells."

The opinions of a youth of 18 could not, however, be finally formed.

(2) *Charles*, known in history as the First of that name, the romance of whose life competes in interest with the untowardly tragical character of its end, confronted by this unfortunate sovereign with dignity and resolution such as has preserved amongst Englishmen abiding respect for the kingly office.

The private woes of the monarch may be faithfully traced, side by side with the errors of his public policy, in those clear, judicial, scientific, and yet kindly, pages of Professor Rawson Gardiner, and beyond recording the dynastic fate of his lineal descendants, this branch of the subject finds no place here.

(3) But it is otherwise with the *third* child of the pedantic Stuart king who crossed the Tweed to govern his country's former foes. *Elizabeth Stuart*, James the First's only daughter, married Frederick, the Elector Palatine, who, posing as Protestant champion, was persuaded by his lovely and chivalrous wife to succour the Bohemian people, then in revolt against the Catholic house of Austria, and, ultimately, to accept the crown offered to him by these revolted populations.

As son-in-law to the King of England, and nephew to Maurice, Prince of Orange, who dominated the United Provinces, Frederick thought he could become the leader of a great Protestant League in Germany. But it was not to be.

Despite the fact that the people of England strained in the leash, and longed to send succour to such of the brave Czechs as were in arms for the cause of Liberty, not only did the British King withhold his approbation from what he deemed rebellion against Ferdinand the Second's authority, but Maurice also, doubting the wisdom of his young relation's romantic project, was unable to do more than send a few regiments to his aid, while 30,000 veteran troops* under Spinola succoured the Emperor Ferdinand, the consequence being, that not only was Frederick utterly defeated at the battle of Prague, in 1620, and lost his ephemeral kingship in Bohemia, but the triumphant Imperialists seized on the Palatinate, and drove Frederick and his fair companion to take refuge in Holland.†

Elizabeth of Bohemia, who suffered so much for the Protestant cause, has a special right to prominence in this record, because in a direct line from that fascinating princess is descended her present Majesty, Queen Victoria, the head of this branch of England's Royal House. The whole narrative reads more like a romance than a tale of sober truth, such as this can be proved to have been.

From the moment when Frederick landed at Gravesend, and proceeded to claim his bride at St. James's Palace, to the fatal day of the catastrophe

* Twenty-six thousand foot and four thousand horse. Rapin, vol. viii. p. 162.

† Hume, vol. vi. p. 104. It is fair to James the First to add that Frederick originally concealed his projects.

at Prague, the young people's lives were spent amidst fêtes and revels, although there were divers anxieties to darken those hopes which to the onlookers seemed so high.

In the first place, the Catholics and Protestants stood divided in political opinion, as they necessarily were in the religious questions, upon which the coming struggle depended, but the additional rivalry of Lutherans and Calvinists, seriously weakened the Prince Palatine's chance of holding his own in Bohemia. Nor should we forget the situation of the Empire, when Frederick accepted the Bohemian crown.

The Emperor Matthias, who died in 1619, had been chosen as a Protestant, and then renounced his opinions, so that the election of a Catholic successor in Ferdinand the Second, occurred when Germany was torn with religious dissensions. The deliberate choice of the Electoral College, arrived at by legal means, was disputed by one of the electorate, who placed himself at the head of the Protestant movement, and, disregarding the majority of his colleagues, as well as the minority both in his own Palatinate and Bohemia, set up the Protestant standard in Prague, and expected to be sustained as king by English and Dutch armies.

We are disposed to attribute the headstrong character of the Prince Palatine's policy to a genuine appreciation of the immense interests at stake when a representative of the Cæsars chosen on religious grounds might hasten to extirpate Protestantism by force of arms, and, if victorious, throw Europe back a century and a half. As a matter of fact the enterprise of Frederick led to the Thirty Years' War, which, despite various fluctuations of fortune, left the Protestants in a far better position than before, when the Treaty of Westphalia closed that struggle in 1648, Catholics and Lutherans being placed on a footing of equality, while six Protestants were to be admitted to the Aulic Council, and equal numbers of each party to be summoned to the Diet, and to have seats in the Imperial chamber.

We recapitulate these facts here because the services to European liberty which Frederick Prince Palatine, and his interesting wife Elizabeth rendered, must be recorded in the very forefront of any chronicle dealing with the history of Her Majesty Queen Victoria's ancestry. The event proved that the unaided strength of Protestantism in South Germany was not sufficient to secure pre-eminence, without the risk of constant anarchical outbursts, incompatible with settled government. On the other hand, James the First of England, playing doubtless for a high stake, if bent on succouring his son-in-law, would have nevertheless entered on a project involving the greatest risk had he sent a contingent to Prague, or even occupied the Palatinate.

It is more a military question than a political one, whether some few thousand (12,000, at most, judging from James the First's after efforts) English troops, for a knowledge of James's resources as to men and transport assures us that a larger force could scarcely have been assembled in Germany, had any chance of turning the scale against so powerful a coalition as was destined to assail and overwhelm Frederick of Bohemia. For the generalship of Maximilian, Duke of Bavaria, quite overshadowed that of the Protestant leaders, even if Spinola had not appeared in Bohemia with his levies from the Low Countries. Indeed, while recognising the sterling qualities of Frederick, brought up as he had been in orthodox Protestant belief, it is impossible to think that he was endowed either with statesmanlike gifts or military faculties.

He was certainly brave, and for the purpose of our story deserves all honour for loyal fidelity and devotion to the noble woman who so cheerfully bore a hard lot in unison with the husband of her choice; and, although destined to be overpowered in the contest, the Palatine was not without allies.

Doubtless the Dutch troops serving with Frederick, and also the few English volunteers, were enthusiastic Protestants, and might have kept an equal force at bay, but they found no adequate support from the Bohemian levies, whose ranks were infected by treachery; so that, despite a gallant resistance, the Imperalists carried all before them.

It was on a Sunday, during morning service, that matters came to a crisis in Prague; and the passage "render unto Cæsar the things which are Cæsar's" came with oracular authority to the congregation at the Lutheran Cathedral, who seem to have held various sympathies. However, in the crash of approaching battle it was impossible to remain in the building, threatened, as it appeared to be, with destruction; so that the preacher left his pulpit, and the people rushed to the Strathoff gate, which led to the field of battle, yclept the White Mountain.

The unfortunate Frederick, who was with his troops outside the city, was cheered at this time by tidings of a check the enemy had received; Marshal Bucquoy's force having been defeated by a wing of the Protestant army.

But soon it became apparent that the Imperialist arms were triumphant outside Prague, and Frederick, galloping to the palace, hurried Elizabeth across to the old town of that name, where, stunned with the calamity, he said, when lifting his wife from the carriage, "I now know where I am. We princes seldom learn the truth until we are taught it by adversity." *

The flight of the ex-King and Queen was followed by the submission of Prague to the Imperial forces, and it soon became evident that the popular voice was with the conquerors, who showed great severity in punishing those who had been in arms for Frederick, that unfortunate prince being placed under the ban of the Empire on January 12th, 1621, and, as a consequence, deprived of his electorship and of the Palatinate which appended thereto.

* Benger's 'Memoirs of Elizabeth Stuart.' Longmans, 1825, vol. ii. p. 90.

The courage of Elizabeth of Bohemia in adversity proved her to be a worthy granddaughter of Mary Queen of Scots, while her devotion for her husband was only equalled by her grief at the separation entailed when Frederick set out from Holland by sea *en route* to Count Mansfeldt's camp in Alsace, which he reached by travelling through France, after landing at Calais.

In Paris he appears to have travelled unknown, to become a silent gazer on the splendid Court of Louis the Thirteenth, and passing on to Hagenau, north of Strasburg, he conferred with Mansfeldt.

But the struggle which ensued was purposeless as regards regaining possession of the Palatinate, inasmuch as the successes of the Imperialists forced Mansfeldt to retreat to his magazines at Hagenau, while the brave Christian of Brunswick failed to effect a junction with his allies. Christian was nevertheless moved to devote his life to the cause of Protestantism in the Palatinate when he beheld Elizabeth Stuart in Holland at the close of the campaign, and he faithfully kept his promise.

The occasion to which we allude was at the Hague, after the battle of Fleurus, when Christian appeared before the ex-Queen of Bohemia with a silver arm in lieu of one amputated on the field.*

* In crossing the Duchy of Luxemburg to relieve Bergen-op-Zoom, Christian's army was attacked by the Spaniards, under Gonzages de Cordova, on the plain of Fleurus, August 30, 1622. This conflict resulted indecisively.—Rapin's 'History of England,' vol. viii. p. 227, quoting Coke Wilson's 'History of Bohemian Rebellion.'

Touched by her grace and cheerfulness under misfortune, Christian is said to have plucked a glove from Elizabeth's hand and placed it in his Spanish hat as a plume, swearing never to lay down arms until he should see the Palatinate returned to its owners. Formerly the stern Duke had placed on his banner, "God's friend, the foe to priesthood." After his interview with Elizabeth it was transformed into "For God and for her."

After a life of privation and danger, wherein he saw the cause he championed steadily worsted, the bluff old Duke Christian of Brunswick, as has already been said, died of fever at Wolfenbüttel Castle, rejoicing that he had rejected the Imperial pardon, and regretting that he had not sealed his pledge given to the ex-Queen of Bohemia with his blood.* Truly a worthy descendant of Henry the Lion, and a hero whom Thomas Carlyle would have delighted to honour.

It is an easy thing to shower blame upon James the First's shoulders for not immediately succouring his daughter; but the best furnished historian who has examined the situation records his conviction that the means adopted after deliberation by the English King, viz. the allying other powers to bring strong pressure on the Empire, was preferable to hasty and single-handed interference such as James could have alone effected. The fault lay in

* Benger's 'Memoirs of Elizabeth Stuart.' Longmans, 1825, vol. ii. p. 236.

the hesitation evinced when diplomacy ought to have retired in favour of action.*

From time to time it appeared likely that Frederick would recover the Palatinate. After Prince Charles and Buckingham returned in haste from Spain, King James the First consented, in 1624, to equip an expedition for the purpose. His troops were promised a free passage through France, according to an understanding with that Court. So it came to pass that 12,000 infantry and 200 cavalry were collected together on ships which rode at anchor outside Calais, until disease broke out amongst the soldiers, and Count Mansfeldt deemed the small force remaining insufficient for such a distant campaign as that in the Palatinate. The worry of the preparation seems to have harassed the peacefully-disposed British King in his last hours, as he died the year following this sad fiasco.

Between this period and the potent advocacy of Gustavus Adolphus, Frederick lost his promising son Henry Frederick, by drowning, in the Zuyder-zee, where father and son had gone together to see the Spanish galleons captured by Peter Heins.†

The yacht which carried the ex-Prince Palatine and his son went down after collision with a larger ship, and Frederick, clinging to a rope, saw his child sink after crying "Save me, father, save me!"

* 'England, Prince Charles, and the Spanish Marriages.' By Prof. Samuel Rawson Gardiner, vol. ii. p. 67.

† Benger's 'Memoirs of Elizabeth Stuart,' vol. ii. p. 260.

Neither Frederick nor Elizabeth were the same people after this tragedy, and the dark shadow thrown over their lives must have prepared Frederick's friends for his own end, which occurred at Metz on November 17th, 1632, eleven days after Gustavus Adolphus had alike triumphed and died in the cause to which they were jointly devoted.

The last days of the widowed Queen were not only embittered by sorrow, but burdened by poverty.

Her brother Charles of England's misfortunes precluded him from stretching out a helping hand, while the presence of the Princes Rupert and Maurice in the royal camp alienated those Puritan sympathies which had been devotedly given to Elizabeth ever since her arrival in Holland. No longer deemed "the pearl of Great Britain," the assistance doled out by the Dutch Government was not granted to her in the same spirit as of yore.

True it is that by the Treaty of Westphalia in the year 1648 her son Charles Lewis recovered the lower Palatinate, taking with him to Heidelberg his young sister Sophia, who was born shortly before Frederick's last expedition into Germany with Gustavus in 1632; but he found the Palatinate in an exhausted condition, and was unable to aid his mother according to her needs or his desires, although he ultimately sent her timely succour.

Concerning the destiny of that gifted lady, the Electress Sophia, it will be ours to tell shortly; and indeed the whole Palatine family story is of such deep concern to one who endeavours to present an outline of Brunswick history, that nothing but the dire necessity of confining these records within a small space leads us to bring this portion of the subject to its close, simply recording how, thanks to the princely liberality of Lord Craven after the Restoration, Elizabeth of Bohemia spent her declining life in comfort such as comported with her dignity. Lord Craven is said to have been her second husband.

First at Drury House, on the site of Drury Lane Theatre, the Earl's seat in London; and finally at Leicester House—destined to be occupied by George the Second when Prince of Wales, and by his son Frederick, who bore this title to his death in 1752—did this noble lady quietly pass her time, while the dissipations and convivialities of the Restoration concerned her not; so that, unnoticed by the revellers, and not noticing them, the "Queen of Hearts" of James the First's Court expired at the latter residence on February 13th, 1662.

How different a fate might have awaited this nation, if James the First had in the first instance risked a heavy stake on restoring the Palatinate, and had succeeded in installing his son-in-law permanently in Prague!

Would the statesmen of England still have chosen this Brunswick dynasty to reign over us? or would not their predominance in German affairs have precluded the accession of which we are writing?

So far the counsels emanating from Windsor in reference to the fortunes of this poor Stuart Princess. But it is a strange thought that strikes the imagination when pondering over the story we have told in bare outline.

Little did James the First think, when with sorrow he allowed his fugitive child to step down from her high estate, that the elder branch of his family should pass through times of sorrow, regicide, and revolution, the ashes of their descendants resting at St. Peter's in Rome; while that helpless widowed Princess, almost forgotten at home amidst the terrors of civil war and rebellion, was destined to become the mother of a famous English dynasty, the progenitrix of five kings, and of a Queen whose name mankind will honour for all time.

Sir Henry Wotton, the poet and diplomatist of James the First's time, regarded the Princess Elizabeth with a chivalrous admiration which found expression in tender verse. He once told her in prose, after her disastrous experience in Bohemia,—"You have showed the World that though you were born within the chance, yet you were without the power of fortune."

The following stanzas speak for themselves:—

"You Violets that first appear,
By your pure purple mantle's known,
Like the proud Virgins of the year,
As if the Spring were all your own;
What are you when the Rose is blown?

"So, when my Mistriss shall be seen
In Form and Beauty of her mind,
By Vertue first, then choice, a Queen,
Tell me if she were not designed
Th' Eclipse and glory of her kind?" *

Charles the First had a high opinion of his sister's ability, and in reference to poor Frederick the Prince Palatine, always said, "The grey mare was the better horse." Moreover, Anne of Denmark, James the First's Queen, never approved of her daughter's marriage, looking upon the Palatinate as an inferior principality and its ruler as a pinchbeck prince. She saw no further than her august husband.

Having dealt with the counsels of Windsor and their influence on posterity, let us now consider how the Brunswick succession to the British throne received a constitutional status.

When James the Second left the country in 1688, a convention parliament declared the throne to be vacant by the absence of the sovereign, and his son being unjustifiably ignored as illegitimate, the Princess of Orange became the recognised heiress, such right to be enjoyed in unison with her husband, whose action in delivering the nation from James the Second's designs was straightway rewarded by the crown. The succession—this single deviation excepted—was vested, first, in the children of Mary; secondly, in Anne and her issue; thirdly, in the lineal descendants of William, who being the son of

* Poems by Sir Henry Wotton, Edition 1845, p. 14.

Mary, eldest daughter of Charles the First, was himself no obscure cadet of the Royal Family.

The first parliament of William and Mary confirmed this settlement, in 1689; but the childless William, anxious for maintenance of the Protestant line so far as Act of Parliament could provide, formulated his project for continuing the succession in the person of the Princess Sophia and her issue, and entrusted his parliamentary proposal in the first instance to Bishop Burnet.

Being carried without opposition in the Lords, this amendment to the Bill of Rights—for it was so entitled—met with opposition from a combination of extreme Whigs, high Tories, and Jacobites in the Commons, who rejected it because they declared it to be unjust to preclude members of the family prior in lineal descent from succeeding to the crown *if they turned Protestant.** The birth of the Princess Anne's son, the Duke of Gloucester, having removed the immediate apprehensions of those who dreaded a disputed succession, a clause was annexed to the Bill of Rights which excluded all Papists from the throne, and also those who should marry Papists; so that when the Duke of Gloucester died, William the Third found no constitutional difficulty in proposing the Brunswick Accession after the Princess Anne and her possible heirs should have passed away.† But the weak point in this settlement became ap-

* Coxe's 'Walpole,' vol. i. p. 8.

† Ibid., p. 9.

parent when it was generally known that James the Second's son was neither supposititious, as his enemies assumed, nor married to a Papist. He therefore lay under no disability which conversion to Protestantism, and consequent marriage with a Protestant, would fail to remove, provided that Parliament acquiesced. This accounts for the persistent efforts we trace of unscrupulous partisans to maintain the *warming-pan* legend, and indeed to add to its absurdity by inventing additions. Take, for instance, the following extract from the parliamentary debates.* After speaking with just reprobation of Perkin Warbeck's deception in Henry the Seventh's time, a speaker in the Scottish Parliament gave vent to the following outburst:—

> "The same game is aplaying now. Perhaps some have never read the history, and others have forgot it. No matter, it happened two hundred years ago; but we cannot forget what happened sixteen years ago, when no male issue was like to succeed King James the Seventh (second of England) . . . One at last was said to be born at St. James, June 1688.
>
> "That child died soon after, a second was put in his place, and carried to and nursed up at Richmond; but God thought fit to kill that second child also. Now, my lord, this pretended Prince of Wales is a third child, in whose veins there is not a drop of royal blood. Here is a new Perkin born into the world."

Although the story of James Edward Stuart's being a supposititious child is now well known to have been invented by James the Second's enemies, it is

* 'Parliamentary Debates,' Edition 1741, vol. iv. p. 429. The orator's name is not given, but the scene occurred in the Parliament House of Edinburgh.

necessary, in a history of this description, to explode the whole story decisively by the production of undoubted evidence collected by the Brunswick family themselves :—

"Quite late in the day, and but a short time before she died in 1714, the Princess Sophia took measures to strengthen the claim which parliament had given her family to the British throne. She was in favour of sending her grandson to England as Duke of Cambridge, and also made searching inquiries as to the question of the Pretender's birth. The warming-pan story still had its votaries, and the truth must at all hazards be known. One Dr. Hugh Chamberlen, a London physician, employed by the court when at St. James's, was consulted, and wrote an important and curious minute relating to events which, though they had happened twenty-six years before, still remained apparently fresh in his memory. He tells Robethon that on 9 June, 1688, he was suddenly called away professionally to Chatham, and on his returning the following day a messenger summoned him in hot haste to St. James's Palace. There, he says, he found 'a child newly born, loose and undressed, in Lady Powys' lap, and as I was told brought forth an hour before I came. I was not long in the chamber when the late Dr. Hamilton came, and then Lord Arran. The Duchess of Monmouth having some time before sent for me, and having in the meantime gone to the Queen's levy, left order I should wait for her grace's return. She was pleased to make this return for her waiting, that she had been with her Majesty.' The evidence that the duchess proceeded to give was of a character to satisfy the medical mind, and its reproduction is unnecessary, as the facts stand recorded in the published accounts of the inquiry which ensued. Dr. Chamberlen concludes in words which must have satisfied the Electress, 'I take the birth to be genuine, without artifice or disguise, so that I never since questioned it.' Moreover he urged that being a 'notorious whig,' he would never have been sent for if a supposititious child had been brought to St. James's. The risk of discovery would have been too great. The outcome of this conversation was totally to discredit the warming-pan theory, which no official adherent of the house of Hanover adduced.*

"Dr. Chamberlen continues, 'The King coming through the Park to St. James's next morning, he was pleased to tell me that when he sent I was absent; to which I humbly replied, more warning had been necessary, but he told me they were surprised, for the Queen expected to go a fortnight longer.' James II. and Dr. Chamberlen then entered into a general conversation on the subject of the birth of children, which it would be tedious to repeat here, unless for the curious admission made by the doctor that 'he believed the science of medicine to be in its infancy.'" *

The Succession was finally decided in favour of the House of Brunswick, the debates thereon having been sparsely attended; and after the Session had been closed by William on June 24, 1701,† the Earl of Macclesfield was despatched to Hanover to apprise the Electress Sophia of her constitutional prospects. The deaths both of James the Second and William the Third followed closely, during this eventful year, and Queen Anne, the incoming sovereign, was at once compelled to sustain a new conflict with the French, whose sovereign scouted the British Queen's title and acknowledged the Pretender as James the Third.

One protest against the Act of Succession deserves mention. It was that of the Duchess of Savoy, grand-

* The letter from which this statement is taken was found in M. Robethon's cabinet, and is amongst the Hanover papers. The summary given here is identical with that in an article of the author's in the 'English Historical Review,' vol. i. p. 768.

† Sir John Bowles, said to be disordered in his senses, was the man chosen to propose the Electress Sophia.—Burnet's 'History of his own Times.' Edition 1838, p. 683.

daughter of Charles the First. Rumour, however, has it that all chance of that branch asserting any claim likely to be heeded had passed away in 1696, when the Duke of Savoy deserted the alliance against Louis the Fourteenth, of which William the Third was life and soul. It is difficult to believe that the great Protestant champion would have ever consented to treat with the Prince of Savoy about family claims to the English throne, unless security was forthcoming in the matter of religion; but we give the statement that the English King had been then prepared to consider the question, for what it is worth.*

* 'The Electress Sophia and the Hanoverian Succession,' by Prof. A. W. Ward, 'English Historical Review,' vol. i. pp. 484, 485. Professor Ward quotes Herr Klopp's 'Fall d'Hauses Stuart,' vol. vii. pp. 74, 75.

CHAPTER IV.

GODOLPHIN AT THE TREASURY, MARLBOROUGH IN THE FIELD.

A.D. 1702–1710.

SYDNEY GODOLPHIN, the Lord Treasurer of the great Administration which bore his name, boasted a varied official experience, and was the man trusted alike by those who ruled the city world, and by Marlborough, the military colleague, who may be said to have acted the part of Foreign Minister to the Government, as well as that of Commander-in-Chief. Monied men felt confident that while Godolphin was at the Treasury and pursued the war with France, they would continue to receive a large percentage on their capital invested in the funds,* while Marlborough took his friend's pre-eminence in council as an earnest of regular remittances for payment of soldiery and purchase of necessaries for the camp. In fact, he made it a *sine quâ non* that Godolphin must be at the Treasury if he were to remain at the head of the army. Godolphin had been a page at

* 'Letters of the Duchess of Marlborough,' Ed. 1742, p. 145.

Charles the Second's Court, and the merry Monarch said of him that "he was never in the way, and never out of it."* Later in the above reign, and when holding the Treasurer's staff, Godolphin had favoured the exclusion of the Duke of York, afterwards James the Second, from the throne, in consequence of his Papistical leanings; but nevertheless, when the time came, the practised official cheerfully served James, even though he was called on to resign the Treasury to Lord Rochester; and it is rumoured that this indispensable minister had tender feelings for Mary of Modena, which were contracted when chamberlain to her household.† Be that as it may, such admiration for the ex-Queen—and it has not been suggested that the sentiment implied anything not purely Platonic—did not prevent him from occupying the position of Treasury Commissioner under William the Third, who recognised his business talents, and benefited by his sagacity.

Finally we see him elevated to the Premiership under Anne, and destined to head the Administration which rendered her reign for ever glorious in our military annals.

In every age and amidst every race there are individuals of only fair or even of ordinary capacity, who, without displaying any one conspicuous talent, nevertheless possess some special faculty which enables them to shine beyond their fellow-men.

* Macaulay's 'History of England,' vol. i. p. 255.

† Ibid., p. 255.

No striking speaker, nor yet qualified in other ways to stir the imaginations of his countrymen, Godolphin rendered himself necessary to each consecutive sovereign under whom he lived, because, in the great Duke of Wellington's words used nearly a century and a half later, he understood how to carry on the Queen's Government. This faculty was never more in demand than when the Earl of Marlborough —for he had not yet won his Dukedom—undertook to conduct the war in Flanders. Of Marlborough much need not be said, as his life, in outline at least, is necessarily familiar to every educated Englishman. It is however to be regretted that it is necessary in the pursuit of truth to reveal certain acts of duplicity as regards the Succession of which this gifted soldier and able diplomatist was guilty. Yet these animadversions will not imply any sympathy with the bitter and unreasonable literary attacks to which the Duke was exposed by contemporary writers. Such lapses from the path of integrity are rather to be charitably lamented than harshly condemned, for the extremely difficult position of English statesmen at that period should be borne in mind before the reins are given to merciless censure. The very wisest masters of affairs were then unable to forecast the immediate future, and could not be sure that they might not at an hour's notice be all attainted exiles, or even condemned prisoners, because they championed the dynastic cause which appeared to themselves that of law, order, and liberty. Under such temptations most men succumbed. All praise then to the honoured names of Somers, Halifax, and Cowper, who never flinched, which, alas! must be regretfully withheld from John Churchill, the great Duke of Marlborough. But Englishmen will strive to forget political conduct which they cannot condone in contemplation of that stroke of genius which led to the campaign of 1704, having its scene of action on the Danube, rather than, as the enemy expected, on the Meuse or Rhine; while it will also be well to remember that when Marlborough crossed swords in 1709–10 with Villars—rightly called the saviour of France by reason of his subsequent victories — the laurels were apportioned to the British general, not to that remarkable commander whose memory is so fondly treasured in France. No—like Vendôme and Tallard before him — Villars was destined to feel Marlborough's superiority.

The capture of Mons after the bloody battle of Malplaquet, in September 1709, vies with the strategic success which saved Arras in 1710, in demonstrating the pre-eminence which we claim for the premier captain in an age of warriors whose campaigns are studied and admired wherever military science flourishes.

There is a political incident generally known to readers of history, but of which the importance is still not sufficiently realised, viz. that Lord Godolphin was Minister up to the opening of William the

Third's last parliament, but then resigned his office of Lord Treasurer because he had objected to the dissolution which preceded the election in question.* Hence there occurred an interregnum between the régime under which the Brunswick Succession was voted, and that which predominated when the famous Godolphin-Marlborough Government commenced their glorious career. Lord Carlisle held the famous White Staff in that Cabinet which attainted the son of James the Second, and received as colleagues Sir Charles Hedges and Lord Manchester. But when the new Queen's accession was followed by the elevation of the Duke of Marlborough to the position in her public counsels which he and his wife had long held in private, Godolphin was again chosen, much against his will, to steer the ship of state. Now at this period of his career, whatever his prescience, however adroit his political address, Queen Anne's first Minister was in private sympathy with St. Germain. During the years 1696, 1697, a Colonel Sackville had acted as intermediatory between the exiled Stuarts and this celebrated statesman; while in 1701 the secret correspondence of Marlborough and Godolphin was carried on through one Berry; and it is impossible not to believe, after carefully sifting memoranda the purport of which has never been denied, that the assurances formerly given to James the Second were renewed to his son in 1702,

* These facts are clearly set forth in the continuation of Sir James Mackintosh's History, Edition 1839, vol. ix. p. 138.

when the statesmen concerned in these negotiations were about to rule over England.*

On the other hand, among the Record Office papers of the period, one finds again and again notices of the haunts frequented by Jacobite and Jesuit priests, such people being hunted for their lives, as if accounted veritable vermin by the authorities who held sway under the ever-religious, ever-Protestant Queen Anne. Those very records, however, disclose what we believe to be the key to this difficult problem.

But the contest between Whig and Tory in the British Parliament was assuming new proportions. The secret diffusion of their principles by the irresponsible Whig junto, of which Lord Somers was chief, had slowly but surely taken effect on the constituencies which, even in the least popular form, and in days of undue electoral restriction, as well as of semi-legalised corruption, yet reflected more or less the popular will. Moreover, the recent Tory proposal to allow the next heir to enter the kingdom, and take up a position near the throne, had neither been in accordance with the Queen's prejudices, nor did it find a response in the prevalent opinions concerning the Succession. The nation was not enthusiastic for any ruler from beyond seas, but was easily

* "Your late conference with Counsellor Gilburn (Godolphin) doth in a good measure clear the suspicion of his and his party's being joined with Hanmer (Hanover) against Matthews (the King)."—Macpherson's 'Original Papers,' vol. i. p. 609. August 21, 1702.

Marlborough's cant names were Malbranche and Armsworth.

moved to anger against the Pope, Priests, and Jesuits. Thus the dominant feeling was subject to divers influences that statesmen could not pretend to control, and the *vox populi* uttered an uncertain sound through all these transactions; so that the Whigs might well congratulate themselves when the triennial parliamentary election of 1705 showed an increased number of Low Church or Whig representatives, while the choice of Mr. Smith as Speaker proved that Lord Godolphin's necessities, if not his sympathies, were leading him to cast the balance against his former Tory allies.

For the moment Harley's schemes were apparently checkmated, although an underground wire-puller has such a singular advantage in deciding when and where he shall commence the game again, that it is impossible to be sure that the hour of apparent defeat is not in truth a mere lull in the attack of the assailant, who straightway devising another operation nearer the fortress, saps his way onwards unobserved and unhindered. Such at least was the method of Harley, the adroit and able party-leader whose nobler qualities were lost in the unworthy tactics then more or less in vogue, and which he ever employed. We are not concerned here to trace successively the steps of intrigue by means of which the whole Whig junto gradually gained places in Godolphin's Government, although they were nevertheless in like manner slowly but surely pulled down from their hardly-gained posts by Harley after he and his brilliant colleague St. John had been dismissed in 1708.* Incredible as it may appear, when acting as leaders of the Whig party, and as late as the close of the year 1706, both Godolphin and Marlborough undoubtedly offered assurances to the St. Germain Court, although several modern historians either explain them away, or ignore them altogether.

It is worthy of record that during a debate on a proposal to better secure her Majesty's person and the Protestant succession, which passed the House of Commons in 1705, one Mr. Charles Cæsar standing up in his place used the following words :—

> "There is a noble Lord, without whose advice the Queen does nothing, who in the late reign was known to keep up a correspondence with the Court at St. Germain"—

words bearing evidence that subordinate politicians suspected what has now become notorious to those who chose to learn the truth. After a scene and a renewed debate, Mr. Cæsar, who had been withdrawn from the House, was committed to the Tower,† and suffered a lengthy imprisonment. Towards the end of 1708, an act of grace was passed which expressly pardoned all previous correspondence with the Jacobite Court, and according to a rumour, which found its way into Mr. Carte's Memorandum-book, and is endorsed by Macpherson,‡ Lord Godolphin

* 'Dictionary of National Biography,' vol. i. p. 459 ("Queen Anne," by Prof. A. W. Ward).

† 'Parliamentary Debates,' vol. iv. p. 492.

‡ Macpherson's 'Original Papers,' vol. ii. p. 104.

had previously been subject to the Whig junto in a very peculiar way. It appears that Lord Wharton had become possessed of an original letter of the Lord Treasurer's to the Pretender's Ministers, and used this document to obtain the Lord-Lieutenancy of Ireland, which Lord Godolphin did not refuse, because not only did this letter keep him at the mercy of the Whig junto, but public curiosity had been aroused by Mr. Cæsar's statement. Lord Wharton was induced to depart to Ireland before the session closed, and the first news he received was of the aforesaid act of grace, by which he knew that the Minister had got himself out of his clutches.*

It is surprising how cautious Lord Godolphin seems henceforth to have been, for during the last two years of his administration, and although Marlborough expressed as usual "zeal and concern" unlimited,† there is no trace of the first Minister having been approached by the Jacobite agents. James the Second advanced the theory that Marlborough and Admiral Russell were encouraged by William the Third in their early communications with St. Germain, in order that through them he might gain information about his foes.‡

Godolphin lives in history as the author of the union between England and Scotland, and very early in his administration seems to have realised

* Hamilton's 'Transactions,' p. 111. The author of the 'Continuation of Sir J. Mackintosh's History' also tells this story. Vol. ix. p. 225.

† Hamilton's 'Transactions,' p. 129.

‡ Clarke's 'Life of James II.,' vol. ii. p. 523.

the necessity of bringing about some such change, the alternative being the tradition of magazines, fortresses, and resources to an irreconcilable foe. He would be a bold man who, after reading of the various projects of invasion intended to be levelled by France and the Pretender with Scotland as a basis of operations, could aver that the Act of Union passed in 1707 did not alter entirely the conditions of such conflicts. It is noteworthy that at this moment a desire to promote Union in these islands seized the people of Ireland, who by the mouth of their Lord Lieutenant, the Duke of Ormond, prayed for a Union between England and Ireland as a fit and just accompaniment of the healing policy pursued with regard to Scotland. The reply sent by Godolphin's cabinet, then in the days of its early strength, was not creditable; as the poor Irish were refused their plea because England declined to share the wool trade with their manufacturers.*

As regards the Scotch Union, whether Godolphin was prompted by the Whig junto or not, he was carrying out the well-known desire of the late King. Through some unaccountable oversight, William the Third had failed to provide for the necessary unity as regards succession to the crowns; and the Scotch Parliament being, on the whole, averse to the Brunswick family, found ready sympathy amongst that intensely national people north of the Tweed, a majority of whom were undoubtedly for restoring

* Hill Burton's 'Reign of Queen Anne,' vol. iii. pp. 144, 145.

their old Stuart kings. The nation protested almost with unanimity against Union; and this, although a majority of the Presbyterians might recoil against the papistical surroundings which James Edward never pretended to forsake.

The national feeling took shape in Edinburgh in popular tumults when the independence of their legislature was threatened; while in the provinces the same feeling prevailed. At Dumfries, during the year 1706, the Articles of Union were burnt, many thousands assembling in the market-place to hail the ceremony with cheerful acclamations. A military force was present—double squadrons of horse and foot surrounding the fire;* but the troops manifestly sympathised with the mob.

The spokesmen who gave voice to this ebullition of patriotic resentment were various. Accepted as a leader by reason of his friendship for Queen Anne, and also for her exiled brother, the Duke of Hamilton comes first on the list. The next place may be given to the Lord Belhaven, whose perfervid oratory is probably better remembered than the more philosophic advocacy of Fletcher of Saltoun—Whig and even Republican in his political belief, but still, as a Scotchman, irreconcilably hostile to the proposed Union. The Parliament hall rang and rang again with the echoes of indignant declamation. The Duke of Hamilton surpassed himself, and waxed so eloquent, that Scotchmen accepted his leadership with content.

* 'Parliamentary Debates,' vol. v. p. 57.

The Highland chieftains, who held their clans under strict, if rude, military discipline, offered the Duke to march on Edinburgh and disperse the parliament if it acceded to the English Minister's request and passed the Union.* Judge then what dismay, what discontent spread over Highland pass and Lowland pasture, when it was known that the National leader had hesitated, and failing to appear in his place in parliament when the crucial struggle was renewed, had abandoned himself to despondence. He had received a letter from Lord Middleton, Secretary of State to the Court of St. Germain, ordering him, on behalf of his master, "to forbear giving any further opposition to the Union."† The Commis-

* Hamilton's 'Transactions,' p. 41. Another theory, to the effect that the Scotch Union was purchased by the English Government, has been exploded by Dr. Hill Burton, who shows that the secret service money unaccounted for was afterwards restored to the Treasury, with the exception of some paltry travelling expenses paid to indigent Whig members. Lord Stanhope also declared the evidence in question to be flimsy. On the principle, it may be supposed, of a penny received as a consideration being binding in the same degree as if it had been a pound, Mr. Secretary Harley held a different opinion regarding these transactions. In a debate regarding the linen trade, and a proposed duty for thirty-two years on all exports of that article, the Scotch very reasonably objected to such a restriction on their commerce.

"After a long debate Mr. Harley said that he admired the debate should last so long. 'For have not wee (meaning and pointing to other English members) bought them (meaning the Scots) and a right to tax them? And pray for what end did wee give the equivalent?' I took him up and said that I was glad to hear a truth, which I had niver doubted, now publickly brought to light and own'd, for the honorable gentleman acknowledged that Scotland was bought and sold."—Lockhart 'Papers,' vol. i. p. 327.

This being a ministerial declaration, it is no marvel that the idea became prevalent.

† Hamilton's 'Transactions,' pp. 42–44.

sioner, in the meanwhile, seizing a moment when his opponents were in confusion, hurried the remaining Articles through the House, and so was passed the Act of Union between England and Scotland.

Harley, at variance with Godolphin and Marlborough, was driven out of the Government in February, 1708, and took with him St. John, the eloquent leader of the House of Commons, who, after sustaining the strife in Flanders and the contiguous French provinces by urging the officials at home to renewed efforts on behalf of his friend the Duke of Marlborough, had practically closed this portion of his career, leaving the people of England content under a war system which had nevertheless sorely strained the national resources. St. John's successor was no less a personage than the famous Robert Walpole, and the change denotes an epoch when the cleavage between the two parties, Whig and Tory, was more distinct than it had hitherto been in Queen Anne's reign. That is to say, Godolphin and Marlborough were prepared to act without Tory aid, while the situation as regards the Brunswick Succession became more and more hopeful. The reader of history will nevertheless perceive that although Blenheim, Ramillies, and Oudenarde, are looked on as the successes of a Whig Government, these glories never could have been achieved without Tory aid. For did not St. John's advocacy in the senate vie with Harley's efforts in the Council Chamber to render all English-speaking men enthusiasts in the resolve to resist Louis the Fourteenth? Did not Shrewsbury, Nottingham and Somerset lay aside their prejudices and join in the successful effort to make Godolphin's Government national and not partisan? Statesmen called on in after time to administer affairs have envied the political calm which reigned for at least three years after Queen Anne's accession, and have longed to realise a similarly patriotic suspension of party strife.

After the year 1708 the war with Louis the Fourteenth seems to have declined in favour at home. At this time the Whigs made the Brunswick Succession a leading article of their creed, while astute leaders, such as Somers and Halifax, were aware that the gentlemen of England were divided into three parties, one lukewarm towards each claimant to the throne, another intensely Jacobite, and to some degree Catholic, while a third section stood ready to receive the Electress Sophia and her heirs, but differed as to the constitutional procedure to be embraced during Queen Anne's lifetime.*

The Tory party was clearly divided, although in the situation certain elements of uncertainty yet prevailed which gave scope to the peculiar talents of Harley, who even thus early in the day was ingratiating himself with the new Court favourite, Mrs. Masham.

* Such a division of parties is described by Bishop Burnet in that instructive and dignified conclusion to the 'History of his own Times.'

There was a touch of romance even in the undignified Court intrigue whereby Harley regained his political footing. Abigail Hill, the bed-chamber woman who supplanted Sarah Duchess of Marlborough in Queen Anne's affections, had become enamoured of Mr. Masham, groom of the chamber to Prince George of Denmark, but failed apparently to make a kindred impression upon the gentleman. But the adroit Harley, perceiving this, made a virtue of acquainting Mr. Masham, *sub rosa*, of the means whereby advancement in life awaited him, *i.e.* if he married his royal mistress's favourite. The youth rose to the bait, and Harley straightway established himself in the Royal graces, while Mrs. Masham, happy in the accomplishment of her heart's desire, advocated the Tory cause unblushingly. This occurred as early as June 3, 1707, when the Duke of Marlborough proved his delicious ignorance of Court intrigue by answering his wife's indignant apostrophe concerning the new favourite's meddlesome conduct as follows:—

"If you are sure that Mrs. Masham speaks of business to the Queen, I should think you might, with some caution, tell her of it, which would do good. For she certainly must be grateful, and will mind what you say." *

A perfectly delicious trustfulness, more worthy of a mere tyro in politics than of the great Marlborough, who with his clever wife were fast falling from the Royal favour necessary to support any

* Marlborough 'Letters.' Edition 1742, p. 185.

high position, however gained, when Queen Anne was on the throne.

To no member of the Roman Church were the English Court and Ministry prepared to hand over the future of their country, but held the throne to be an heirloom to the eldest Protestant heir of the Royal house, who at the moment of the sovereign's demise was declared her successor by a parliamentary title. Thus Godolphin and Marlborough seem to have believed that the legislative powers of Queen, Lords, and Commons being unlimited, it was open to them to rescind a decision regarding the succession which was based on facts recognised to be true when it was proclaimed, and yet liable to alteration, provided the titular head of the exiled Royal Family should resolve to revert to the faith of his grandfather and embrace the doctrines of the English Church.

If then the "pretended" Prince of Wales had only chosen to change his religion and join the Anglican Church, Parliament could have amended its former decision without affronting the majority of Englishmen. They chiefly desired legality with respect to the title of the sovereign, and freedom of opinion for themselves. The latter they rightly or wrongly thought unattainable with a Catholic King at Whitehall. The House of Hanover, on the other hand, was placed next in the succession, because the principles of its members did not prevent them accepting the theories of Government which the laws of the

English constitution prescribed. Theories these, which, if not expressly recognised in Germany, nevertheless receive practical acknowledgment among all Teutonic peoples, notwithstanding the occasional absence of legal restraint upon autocracy even in its most naked form.*

The right of a man to live within the law has not been threatened beyond the Rhine for two centuries, unless the various divided provinces fell under foreign domination, and it is remarkable that in later years Germany, with its rude and scarcely defined local liberties, defied, comparatively unharmed, the ravages of that marvellous revolution which submerged France after 1792, in spite of the fact that the Grand nation could call at will on an ancient national Parliament, or States-General, which however, having no popular root, exercised comparatively little influence.

So it came to pass that the attitude of the Electress Sophia and that of the Elector George Lewis was purely expectant, though they were not wanting in legitimate ambition. The national feeling in England therefore steadily pointed towards sustaining the decision of William the Third's last Parliament, and although at the beginning of Queen Anne's reign enthusiasm for the family of Brunswick-Luneburg did not exist, and some wise men doubted whether they would ever succeed; still the pre-

* This is commented on by Carlyle in the earlier chapters of his 'Frederick the Great.'

sumption remained in their favour when Godolphin and Marlborough undertook to prosecute the most important war which this country had ever waged in Europe. But men differed as to the scope and design of these operations. For instance, Lord Rochester, the Queen's uncle, leader of the Tories, desired that England should act as an auxiliary, not as a principal, confining warlike operations to the sea, which was even then considered her native element.

However, this small dissension did not prevent Lords Marlborough and Godolphin from forming an administration on the broadest possible lines, the thread that bound men of diverse political sympathies being the general resolve to sustain the war with France. Nor was such unity attained without the cognisance, and consequent warm support, of the so-called Whig junto, amongst whom were Somers, Cowper, Halifax, Townsend, Sunderland—Marlborough's son-in-law—and Wharton, these able statesmen and their associates forming a sort of informal and yet influential outer cabinet whose opinions, regularly formulated, were nevertheless to sway the decisions of official chiefs in every department of the Government guided by Godolphin, and crowned with glory by his coadjutor Marlborough.* Yet another agency existed, the influence of which was felt at each crisis between 1702 and 1710,

* See Harrop's 'Bolingbroke,' p. 28, where commences an able analysis of the subject, to which the writer is much indebted.

namely, the astute policy of Mr. Secretary Harley. This minister was resolved that neither Whig nor Tory should become too strong, so he trimmed and schemed according to circumstances, never exercising his natural powers of intrigue more fruitfully than when in 1704 he introduced the eloquent and energetic St. John into the Ministry as Secretary for War, in which capacity he gave the Duke of Marlborough the valuable support of his unrivalled eloquence. The public spirit was thereby braced up at a juncture when every nerve of the nation was fully strained, and every resource had been laid under contribution.

Moreover, St. John's unflagging industry in the cabinet managed to provide the ways and means needful for carrying on the campaign of 1704 which ended so triumphantly on the field of Blenheim. This success was achieved without hindering the prosecution of the war in Spain. The victory of Blenheim was all the more important, in that no great advantage had been previously gained by the Allies. The campaign of 1702 was satisfactory, to England especially, because thereby Marlborough had been proved a skilful leader. As to the indecisive countermarches and sieges of 1703, if the balance of advantage remained with the English general, yet the final issue of war was still uncertain. Therefore at such a crisis the attraction of the Duke of Savoy to the coalition against France* was valuable, be-

* Macpherson's 'History of Great Britain,' vol. ii. p. 273.

cause not only did he possess a well-appointed army, but his appearance showed a lack of unanimity as to the succession amongst the Roman Catholic members of the Royal House of England.

Another potent ally was gained to the Anglo-Dutch-Imperial cause when the King of Portugal entered the lists as an enemy of Louis the Fourteenth, thus opening a base of attack against Spain, of which a maritime nation such as England was enabled to avail itself. At this time was laid the foundation of a traditional alliance between England and Portugal which preserved the liberty of Europe little more than a century afterwards. The war, notwithstanding St. John's eloquent advocacy, had unfortunately suffered in the estimation of a large section of English politicians when Marlborough was loaded with a premature crop of honours so early in the strife as 1702; for the campaign of that year, although smart and creditable to the general, was not of a character which deserved an acknowledgment as splendid as a Roman triumph. The Earl of Marlborough received on this occasion a Dukedom and a pension of £5000 a-year during life, for baffling Marshal Boufflers, retaking several Belgian towns, and freeing the navigation of the Meuse. But he fought no battle of importance until Blenheim, in 1704.

Godolphin then had to serve many masters when he was ostensible head of the Administration formed to give Marlborough a free hand on the Continent.

Indeed, the Jacobite agents seem to have recognised the difficulties which these two merchants—as Lord Caryll was pleased to style them—were certain to meet with if they elected to pay their old debts. Hence a disposition amongst the adherents of St. Germain to look charitably on Godolphin's lately adopted rôle of comparative silence, while they took for what they were worth Marlborough's more effusive professions of a desire to serve his Queen's brother when opportunity offered.*

The professions alluded to were made only a few months after the Danube had run red with the blood of Englishmen who were avowedly striving to keep this same prince from inheriting the throne of England. Truly a tangled situation, and one which it is impossible to clear of a certain perplexity even when the aims of the various actors in the scene are to some extent disclosed. It has been suggested that Queen Anne herself desired this attitude to be preserved towards the candidature of her brother, and it is clearly true that the ties of close relationship had led her to desire James Edward's conversion to English Church principles, although from beginning to end the last Stuart Sovereign of England stood as defender of the Protestant faith. No more light can be thrown on this phase of the question, so that it

* "I must also own the receipt of yours of the 3rd of May, wherein you relate what passed between you and Mr. Goulton (Godolphin), which merchant is not so prodigal of his words as his partner Armsworth (Marlborough)." Lord Caryll to Lord Middleton.—Macpherson's 'Original Papers,' vol. i. p. 700.

remains to seek a solution of the failure to compromise matters with St. Germain by reciting in the next chapter the facts concerning the old Pretender's religious opinions.

Godolphin, at this period, received notice of Mrs. Masham's intrigues, and also of Harley's proceedings, both "within doors and without." Whigs and Tories were alike cajoled, and an opposition set up to the Government such as neither Marlborough's military success, nor the extreme cleverness of his wife, could prevent from gaining ground. Such was the moment chosen by the advisers of James Edward Stuart to make an attempt on Scotland, which effectually cut off the youth thus pressing his claim to the Scotch throne from any hopes of succeeding with the Queen's good-will to the throne of Great Britain.* It could not be otherwise; and although from time to time the Duke of Hamilton did act as a negotiator between the brother and sister, yet the terms proposed at St. Germain were totally foreign to those which a Protestant Queen could ever think of entertaining, and the Stuart adherents were henceforth destined to pursue a glittering will-o'-the-wisp yclept Restoration. In fact, the whole bent of modern life in England was adverse to the cause of James Edward Stuart. The commercial spirit which William the Third fostered so consistently, and which rendered the Dutch more powerful than their comparatively slender ter-

* See next chapter. He was henceforth officially called the Pretender. —Burnet's 'History of his own Times,' ed. 1838, p. 826.

ritory warranted, was unpalatable to princes and statesmen of the old *régime*, who, in alliance with the Roman hierarchy, still sought to put the world back just so far as suited their pretensions.

But the people of England had chosen to throw in their lot with the party of progress; and remembering how Northern Germany had stood firm in the fight during the Reformation, while Brunswick was ever to the fore, they selected a Protestant princess of semi-Germanic origin, whose blood entitled her to the British throne, in preference to letting it be tenanted by a prince whose followers scoffed at the theological teachings of Luther, and, still worse, in the eyes of men desiring liberty, scouted the toleration of Erasmus.

The history of the United Kingdom is not to be re-written, else several pages might be covered with an interesting dissertation upon the trial of Dr. Sacheverell for tilting at the Prime Minister, Lord Godolphin, and calling him Volpone, in the course of a sermon delivered at St. Paul's on November 5, 1709. This sermon was declared to be seditious, because, when asserting the right divine of anointed sovereigns, it struck at Queen Anne's title to rule over England. The trial that followed ended unsatisfactorily for the Government, as they made a martyr of the extravagant clergyman whose vagaries they noticed, but only found themselves supported by the scant majority of ten in the House of Lords, when combating Sacheverell's assertions to the effect:*—(1) "That the necessary means for effectuating the late revolution (1688) were odious and unjustifiable." (2) "That the toleration of Dissenters was both unreasonable and unwarrantable." (3) "That the Church of England was in danger under the Queen's administration." (4) "That there were persons in office who endeavoured to overturn the constitution, and that, through the whole management of affairs, there was a mal-administration and corruption." †

Strong terms these in which to describe an administration so triumphantly successful as Lord Godolphin's had proved. Indeed, the party proceedings of the Tories on this occasion may be said to have provoked the reprisals from which they suffered when their rivals triumphed at the beginning of the next reign.

The very completeness of Marlborough's victories had given the Ministers a taste for glory such as it was impossible to satiate, and the refusal of England to treat on reasonable terms at Gertruydenberg, in 1710, operated adversely to Lord Godolphin with a large section of the public. Those who concurred in absurd charges, such as those of Sacheverell, hoped thereby to establish a new Ministry in power pledged to conclude peace with France, and so to save the nation's treasure, and husband resources already perilously strained. It was hoped that the main

* The numbers were 69 against, and 59 for Sacheverell.

† Records of the Trial.

objects of the war would be attained by a peace honourable and at the same time durable.

Hence the formation of the Government known in history as Lord Oxford's, although the Treasurer's staff was at the outset placed in commission.

Queen Anne's new advisers could not, on the whole, vie with their predecessors in the matter of ability; yet several characters of celebrity enrolled themselves under the Tory banner, while Harley became Earl of Oxford, and St. John, Viscount Bolingbroke—an advancement which he received with chagrin rather than satisfaction, as he hoped to revive an Earldom which once belonged to his ancient family.

It is impossible not to contemplate these changes, and their assumed effect on the Succession question, without some sympathy for the fallen Minister, Lord Godolphin, who had gradually become a cipher in his own cabinet, obliged to see his friends removed one by one at Harley's instance, until at last he received a curt message from the Queen to break and deliver up the White Staff. In deep resentment he broke it to pieces, and betook himself to his beloved Newmarket, where for the most part he lived until, at the end of two years' time, death removed him from the scene of his notable career.

According to the Jacobite tradition, it is averred that Godolphin declared privately, that he would have restored James Edward Stuart without French aid, but that Lord Oxford would have attempted the same achievement by means of a Bourbon alliance.* But the resolves of this celebrated man as regards the Succession remain at present an impenetrable secret. Marlborough had left for Holland in January, 1710, to confer with Pensionary Heinsius, and take counsel with the Elector of Hanover concerning the next campaign; but his position with reference to the home Government is summed up thus by a remarkable letter of Lord Bolingbroke's, written shortly before he gained his peerage, and of which a copy appears amongst the Hanover papers. It is directed to his friend Mr. Drummond, the banker, and British Resident at Amsterdam, and runs as follows:—

"Whitehall: Jan. 23, 1710.

. . . "As to the great man you mention I have wrote a few but plain words to your Pensionary. He was not received with the acclamations you heard of, and they are much mistaken that imagine that he can be upon any other bottom than that what the Queen pleased to put him.

"I daresay he is convinced by this time that he cannot lead either his mistress or any one else as he used to do. We shall send him over a subject; take care you do not put royalty into his head again.

"Adieu. I am ever with the utmost sincerity,

"Your most obedient servant,

"HENRY ST. JOHN."

It soon became evident that if the new Government was to stand, the chief power must rest with Oxford and Bolingbroke. Rochester, the Queen's uncle, had been gathered to his fathers, and no com-

* It is a remarkable fact that Godolphin wrote no letters to the Court of Hanover, and he is not even mentioned in the Hanover Papers.

petitors on the Tory side could hope to vie with them in management of Parliament or knowledge of affairs.

But we hasten to trace the fortunes of those Stuarts who, by reason of their religion, were precluded from reigning in England.

CHAPTER V.

THE EXILES OF ST. GERMAIN.

Whether it is stranger to contemplate James the Second living at variance with the Pope during the latter part of his reign, just when he was endeavouring to re-establish the Roman Catholic faith, or dying in the very odour of sanctity, so that his remains worked divers miracles, it is difficult to determine.*

But it is certain that Innocent XI. reprobated James's conduct towards England, because it was calculated to advance the Jesuits' influence (ever reprobated by that Pontiff) and increase the power of Louis the Fourteenth, who was engaged in differences with the Pope, which were not in his lifetime composed.

When Bishop Burnet, the very embodiment of a Protestant Whig, retired from England in 1686, he received a courteous reception from the Papal Court,†

* Somers' 'Tracts,' vol. xi. p. 314. Clement XI. promised to offer public prayer in the Pontifical Chapel for the soul of James the Second, and—shade of Innocent XI.!—he spoke of his dear son in Christ, Louis the Fourteenth.

† Burnet's 'History of his own Times,' ed. 1838, p. 423.

the Pope offering him a private audience, and the Cardinals Howard and d'Estrees paying him marked attention. This gracious behaviour towards one of the English King's chief opponents was a straw plainly showing which way the wind blew in the Curia. The course of James the Second in England was, we repeat, not approved of at Rome; while the Papal Secretary Caffoni was actually intriguing with the Dutch against him. The above-mentioned Cardinal d'Estrees wrote, on December 18, 1687, to M. de Louvois, Minister of Louis the Fourteenth, saying that by the joint stratagem of a French spy, one Le Gut, and a clerk of the Papal Secretary by name Le Petit, the following information was discovered on the person of a Dutch burgomaster named Ouir, who had been for some time suspected of intriguing with Caffoni, the Pope's Secretary.

The written instructions of the Emperor, the Duke of Lorraine, and the Prince of Orange to the burgomaster were seized, and therein Le Gut discovered a league against France, which was to take effect on the Rhine, William of Orange taking the command. Caffoni declared in his letters that the Pope was "very glad of this," but in a remote corner of the Dutchman's cabinet was the disclosure—made to Caffoni—that William really intended his expedition to land in England to dethrone James the Second, and place his daughter Mary on the throne. Moreover, a statement was appended that the Holy Father knew nothing of this.

Thus according to Dalrymple,* who gives chapter, book, and verse for the assertion, Innocent's treasury furnished a portion of the funds which enabled William of Orange to dethrone James the Second. The same author produces a letter † from the Protestant leader himself to the Emperor, saying he went to pacify England and not "to make an attempt on the crown." This occurred without the Pope learning anything beyond the current gossip which told how William of Orange was organising a league against Louis the Fourteenth, but could find no support at the Court of St. James's, where the last Stuart king was engaged in projects the success of which depended on friendly neutrality at Versailles.

At any rate, we have presented to us before the Revolution of 1688, the strange spectacle of Rome divided against herself, certainly by reason of the Pope's jealousy of the Jesuits, possibly because intense disapprobation of the French king's conduct concerning his embassy in Rome rendered Innocent blind to the course of events in England,‡ and this

* Dalrymple's 'Memoirs,' vol. ii. p. 121.

† Ibid., vol. ii. p. 132.

‡ This was a revival of a quarrel which broke out immediately after Louis the Fourteenth ascended the French throne. Louis was determined to preserve the right of asylum for his ambassador which the Pope had induced the Emperor, together with the Kings of Spain, Poland, and England, to renounce, and despite his isolation in the matter, this haughty Bourbon sent an armed embassy under the Marquess of Lavardief, and took possession of the Vatican itself, together with the church of St. Louis. Moreover, he insisted on nominating the Elector of Cologne.—'The Age of Louis XIV.,' by Voltaire, English translation, ed. 1779, vol. i. pp. 183, 184.

although after events proved beyond all doubt that the Roman Catholic Church recognised the efforts of James the Second to bring England once more into the fold. Indeed two years had not elapsed before the Papal Court had engaged an historian to recount James's restoration to the British throne,* although these literary preparations were rendered abortive when the battle of the Boyne, in 1690, spread dismay amongst the counsellors of the Vatican. After James's death—as we have stated—Pope Clement XI. made acknowledgment before the College of Cardinals of the indebtedness his Church felt towards the late British King.

James the Second had consistently refused to make terms with the revolution such as might have left his successors a loop-hole through which to escape from their responsibilities to the ancient faith. He decisively declined to concur in the suggestion of Louis the Fourteenth whereby the youth known in history as the Chevalier de St. George, or the Old Pretender, should be placed next in the succession to William and Mary, and stated that he owed it to posterity, as to the English people, not to condone his own deposition or allow James Edward to regain the throne by such means.†

James, with potent arguments on his side, declaimed against the disadvantages of a monarchy

* Stated in Clarke's 'Life of James II.,' quoting Kennet.

† 'Life of James II.,' collected out of memoirs from his own hand, by Rev. J. S. Clarke, Librarian to George IV., vol. ii. p. 571.

purely elective, and ignoring the strong position of that portion of the Royal Family which embraced principles of freedom both in Church and State, he refused to enter into any compromise infringing the right divine of kings. For such adherence to a policy of *thorough*, as regards the form of Christianity which he had chosen, James's memory was held precious by that branch of the Church, and although absolute canonisation was not adopted, his remains, resting in the Benedictine Church at Paris, weathered even the French Revolution itself.

Hidden away from sight by some admirers during that upheaval of society, James's ashes were still unburied when the Allies entered Paris in 1813, and at the command of George the Fourth they were straightway consigned to the tomb at St. Germain, many of the English then in France joining in that strangely delayed procession.*

* Within a few weeks of this work appearing, a coffin containing the heart of James the Second has been found on the site of the Scotch College in Paris—once a great Jacobite centre. According to the Paris Guide-book, to which Victor Hugo wrote a preface in 1848, the presence of this treasure was known at that period, and it had been long prized as a precious relic by the Scotch Catholics, who in former days sent their archives to this retreat. The Scotch College was founded by David Murray in 1326, and remained a resort where the youth of Scotland sought their education until, the Presbyterians overcoming the Roman Catholics at home, many of the latter brought their valuable papers to France for safety. Cardinal Beaton in 1532 anticipated events when, deeming the end of Church tyranny in Scotland was approaching, he deposited various manuscripts in this College.—M. Michel, 'Les Écossais en France,' vol. i. p. 56. The Scotch College was originally situated at St. Geneviève, Rue des Amandiers, and in 1662 was transferred by Robert Barclay a little more to the west, in the Rue des Fosses. It was suppressed in 1792, but the building still stands. In it Saint Just was confined.

Miss Strickland, to whose industry we owe a curious account of the opening of the English King's coffin, speaks of the French people acting in a spirit of iconoclasm towards the dust of their own sovereigns, and yet sparing that of James the Second by reason of some lingering belief in his sanctity. But surely the explanation lies nearer the surface, inasmuch as it was the descendants of Louis Capet, rather than those of the Stuart kings, whom a Paris mob sought to dishonour when crazed with the madness which overtook the French people at the close of the 18th century.*

The last years of the life of James the Second had been spent in comparative seclusion, and he yearly retreated to the Monastery of La Trappe, held occasional converse with superiors of religious conventual houses,† and frequented the great solemnities of the Church in Paris, living not for himself or the world, but preparing, in the manner his religion bade him, for the life hereafter, as a contrite and earnest penitent. No reader of that remarkable paper of advice which he left for the guidance of his son ‡ can fail to recognise the sincerity of the man, but in the strange retrospect there disclosed no word of penitence for his disregard of law and the wishes of a vast majority of his subjects escaped him. On the contrary, he desired to see his son follow in

* Miss Strickland's 'Lives of the Queens of England,' vol. viii. p. 555.

† Clarke's 'Life of James II.,' vol. ii. p. 583.

‡ Published in full at the end of Clarke's 'Life of James II.,' Appendix ii. p. 655.

the fatal path which he himself had endeavoured to tread. For instance, he says :—

> "In the first place serve God in all things as becomes a good Christian and a zealous Catholick of the Church of Rome, which is the only true Catholick and Apostolick Church, and let no human consideration of any kind prevaile with you to depart from her."

Again he writes, "be never without a considerable body of Catholick troops," while liberty of conscience, as James defined it, he desired to settle by a law, so that the expectant subjects might rest assured that their pious sovereign designed not to force them into embracing the Catholic faith. "Our blessed Saviour," writes James, "whipt people out of the temple, but I never heard He commanded any should be forced into it." At the same time he expressed horror of all "Latitudinarians as being for the most part Atheists." The Habeas Corpus Act seems to have been held in special abhorrence by the last Stuart king, who believed that the first Lord Shaftesbury designed it in order that sovereigns might be forced to keep "more troops than they otherwise needed, and so incur unpopularity." A jesuitical mode of proceeding we have not hitherto learned to connect with an acknowledged bulwark of our national liberties.

James deeply regretted the sowing of his own wild oats, and specially warned the Chevalier de St. George against the various temptations incident to his position. Indeed he sorrowfully admits the number and unfortunate character of his liaisons, and urges the avoidance of such errors both on public and private grounds, saying that, when some outspoken foes to monarchy urged an attack on certain disreputable recipients of Royal bounty, Lord Mordaunt, leader of the dissentients in question, said: "By no means, let us rather elect Status for them, for if it were not for them the King would not run into debt, and then would have no need of us."

The ex-King showed a due appreciation of the basis on which the power and prosperity of Great Britain rest when he bade his son "study the trade of the nation, and encourage it by all lawful means, 'tis that which will make you at ease at home, and considerable abroad, and preserve the mastery of the sea, without which England cannot be safe."

Such then were the traditions rife amongst the exiled Stuarts when the unfortunate James Edward became the youthful representative of a sinking cause. He passed his life in an atmosphere wherein ideas of civil liberty never could flourish. Mary of Modena, for instance, the mother of the Chevalier, and ex-Queen of England, stood as the very embodiment of her faith, and left no stone unturned to advance the Roman Catholic religion. Conscientious, true, and refined, she merits the respect which her consistent piety gained for her memory, and the pity which misfortune claims for one who received unjust measure from an adopted country.*

* The propagation of the warming-pan story is specially disgraceful to the partisanship that forged so unfair a weapon.

Still it is obvious that a child brought up under her influence must have been precluded from understanding the theories of Government prevalent in England during the era of progress which the reign of William and Mary inaugurated.

It is easy to form a due estimate of James Edward, known in history as the Old Pretender, as the materials are fully to hand. In the first place, this child of misfortune, ushered into the world amidst the convulsions which rent his father's throne, had not any great endowments of intellect to make up for bodily weakness, and consequent despondency of mind. Hume, speaking of James the Second's misfortunes, partly accounted for their overwhelming character by citing the "middling talents" * of the monarch, who at the crisis of his fortunes required special strength, and more than ordinary tact and acuteness, to preserve a throne enfeebled by the shocks it had received under Charles the First, when it was proved to be assailable, and under Charles the Second, when its supporters connived at an epoch of corruption and immorality.

If, therefore, James the Second, with these average powers alluded to by Hume, wrecked his throne and placed monarchy again in peril, could it be hoped that a son still less adapted by nature to cope with the rough world should succeed in accommodating himself to the exigencies of an extremely difficult position, especially as the preliminary condition of success

* Hume's 'History of England,' vol. viii. ch. 71, p. 306.

involved the surrender of the most sacred principles inspired by his whole training? For all the records of that time prove that the age of unbridled autocracy was, in England at least, for ever closed, and that the King on the throne must thenceforth abide by the laws already made, and concur in all timely change duly determined upon by the Legislature. Yet it is impossible to conceive a prince brought up at St. Germain under the influence of such parents, and in the very shadow of the Court of their patron Louis the Fourteenth, consenting to any such restrictions, or if he accepted timely bondage, not casting off the shackles on the earliest available opportunity.

The touches of character delineated in the next few pages will confirm this view of James Edward Stuart, while they increase his repute as a prince with an English heart, whose disposition was gentle and benevolent, and who might have filled the British throne with credit under different training and circumstances.

James the Second's son was only thirteen years of age when his father died, and the direction of affairs in his Court was ostensibly committed to Lord Middleton, who was a statesman of considerable experience; although Louis the Fourteenth's prompt acknowledgment of James Edward as King of Great Britain, an example followed by Philip, Louis's grandson, who had ascended the throne of Spain, had given the French king a title to be consulted, and had therefore restricted the influence of ordinary English advisers.*

Considerable inconvenience was therefore felt at St. Germain when Lord Middleton, impressed by the last words of his late master, retired from office, and sought advice in a religious house near Paris, that he might satisfy some scruples he still felt, and master the tenets of his new faith. He pleaded that his change of religion would prove unpopular amongst many Stuart adherents in England, so that he remained out of office for a year, during which time, Simon Fraser—afterwards Lord Lovat—(a Scotch outlaw whose character had been well known to James the Second and his advisers in exile) insinuated himself into the confidence of Mary of Modena, by means of the Papal nuncio in Paris. Thus, in the absence of Lord Middleton, the Jacobites were saddled with an agent whose duplicity soon became apparent, for when sent into Scotland, he proceeded to accuse his enemies to the Government there of playing the very rôle he was himself performing, viz. that of agent to the Court of St. Germain.† At the commencement of 1704, Lord Middleton had

* Lord Macaulay's 'History of England,' vol. v. p. 289, recounts how this policy of acknowledging James Edward was resolved on when Louis the Fourteenth met Madame de Maintenon returning from St. Germain after visiting the afflicted family of James the Second when that royal exile was dying. The Ministers were one and all against this recognition, but Louis and the French princes thought otherwise. It should not be forgotten that James was their kinsman. M. de Torcy, the responsible Minister at the Court of Versailles, objected to the recognition because it would involve violation of the treaty of Ryswick.

† Macpherson's 'Original Papers,' vol. i. p. 640.

returned to his post of Jacobite Minister, and straightway unveiled Fraser's villainy, henceforth remaining a necessary adviser until the youth, who inherited his father's empty title, could share in the family deliberations.

When the exiled prince was only eighteen years old, the question arose how to interest the victorious King Charles the Twelfth of Sweden in the cause. The Anglo-Imperial armies were pressing Louis the Fourteenth hard; Blenheim, fought in 1704, being followed in May, 1706, by Ramillies, and a march of the foe on Paris seemed likely to reward the chivalrous but impolitic conduct of the French sovereign when he defied England by the acknowledgment of James the Third. The Swedish king, on the other hand, dethroned King Augustus of Saxony, and, annexing his dominions, had rendered himself the arbiter of the North, whence, by threatening the dominions of the Elector of Hanover, and endeavouring to separate them from England,* he might at least create a diversion and give Louis the breathing space he sorely needed. These machinations were however defeated by the temperate diplomacy of the Elector of Hanover, the rival candidate to James Edward for the English throne.

According to the author of Hamilton's 'Transactions,' the first personal intervention of the Old Pretender in politics occurred during the year 1707, when, the Union hanging in the balance, the Scotch

* Macpherson's 'Original Papers,' vol. ii. p. 23.

Parliament was left to make a decision in the absence of the Anti-Unionist leader—the Duke of Hamilton —who, mysteriously absenting himself when the crisis arrived, was said to be following instructions sent by James Edward in a letter from St. Germain. This policy is so contrary to that generally enjoined on the Scotch friends of the House of Stuart, at the epoch in question, that it is impossible not to doubt the allegation as yet unsupported by further evidence —the more so that when Colonel Hooke, the Jacobite agent, visited Scotland in 1708, he looked to the house of Athol rather than that of Hamilton to produce a leader for his master's party. Moreover, Macpherson has tendered evidence of the latter Duke's unpopularity at this period. On the other hand, it should not be forgotten that if the Duke of Hamilton was the friend of James Edward Stuart, so was he notoriously the servant and associate of Queen Anne, from whom he may have taken his orders.

There was, however, no antecedent improbability that the Pretender should intervene in the conduct of his own affairs, because on June 28, 1706, Lord Middleton had written to M. de Torcy as follows:—"The King, my master, applies to business now, with the address of a skilful workman."* One signal result of this hard work carried on in concert with the advisers of his mock Court, was the attempt made to invade Scotland at the commence-

* Macpherson's 'Original Papers,' vol. ii. p. 4.

ment of the year 1708, a venture extorted from the French Ministry by repeated and earnest solicitations.*

Louis the Fourteenth might have stood excused from making this attempt at all, even from the standpoint of royal patron, as the iron grasp of the Allies was tightening upon his frontier, and rendered it impossible to send more than an inadequate force of between four and five thousand men to promote this haphazard but not premature invasion.† Yet in spite of the distresses of Louis the Fourteenth the scheme of Jacobite invasion was not by any means hopeless. At this juncture, Scotland, discontented with the Union, was eager to fly to the Prince's standard, while the Government had scarcely five thousand men available north of the Tweed, the remainder being in the Low Countries.

Louis the Fourteenth appears to have believed that he might create a diversion in his own favour by means of this expedition, by forcing Marlborough to take troops to England from Flanders, even if the main object was foiled,‡ and the Chevalier gained no footing across the channel. And had the French admiral, Forbin, with only five ships, not met his British opponent, Admiral Byng, with sixteen, off the coast of Fife, these hopes might have been justified. One of Forbin's ships, the *Salisbury*, had

* Macpherson's 'Original Papers,' vol. ii. p. 98.

† 'Lockhart Papers,' vol. i. p. 238.

‡ Stanhope's 'Reign of Queen Anne,' p. 340.

passed too far up the Firth of Forth, and was captured, having on board, the aged Lord Griffin, and two sons of Lord Middleton,* but the rest of the French vessels made good their escape northwards.

This important capture might have been expected to rejoice the English Government, instead of which it seemed to be regarded by them rather in the light of an embarrassment. Lord Middleton's two sons were soon released, by order of the Queen, and it has been said that their father was in possession of compromising evidence that Godolphin had corresponded with the Court of St. Germain.† Lord Griffin, on the other hand—an aged and weak-minded man, already outlawed for complicity in Jacobite designs—was allowed to drag out the rest of his life

* The following list, to be found among the undated papers at the Record Office, Queen Anne, Domestic Series, of those taken prisoners on the *Salisbury* in 1708, will be of interest:—

"Her Majesty's subjects taken on board the *Salisbury*:—Le Sieur de Beaufort, Captn. au Regiment de Bearn—gone to Nottingham to the other French prisoners; Edmund Fitzgerald, aid de camp; Daniel Mcharty, Lieu.; Stephen Conner, Do.; Edmund Fitzgerald, Do.; Michael Prendergast, Do.; Terence MacMahon, Do.; Oliver Bourk, Do.; Daniel Bailey, Anthony Stand Burke, Peter Bruilly, Servants gone to the Tower with Lord Griffin and his servant; Mr. Denovan, Lieut. of Foot; Mr. Hynes, Do.; Mr. Fannon; Mr. Macarty; Mr. O'Sullivan; Mr. Fitzmorris; Mr. Cleary and two servants." Marshal Martignon's own account of the affair may be of interest:—"I discoursed with M. de Fourbin, to know of him, whether having missed our landing in the Firth of Edinburgh, we might not attempt it in another place. He proposed to me Inverness, which is a very remote part in the north of Scotland, and we went immediately to speak of it to the king of England, who entertained the motion with joy." —Letter of Marshal Martignon to M. de Chamillard, Minister of Louis XIV., Rapin's 'History of England,' vol. xvi. p. 543.

† Hamilton's 'Transactions,' p. 90.

in the Tower, an exercise of mercy which gave dissatisfaction to the Whig junto.*

Altogether it is impossible not to think that Queen Anne's Government was threatened on this occasion with a danger of untold magnitude. But fortunately the peril was averted, for the most part in consequence of the elements proving unpropitious, while Forbin's final refusal to put the Chevalier ashore in the Inverness Firth, notwithstanding that Marshal Martignon, the commander of the French land-forces, concurred with James Edward as to the desirability of the venture, at once blighted every remnant of hope.

The sorrow of this unfortunate son of James the Second as he left behind him the Ross-shire mountains and lost sight of the distant towers of Inverness, can be scarcely exaggerated, but was probably surpassed by the dull sense of failure and despondency which must have oppressed his heart as he sighted Dunkirk, doubtless remembering how Louis the Fourteenth had there so lately expressed a desire never to see him again.†

"Had this expedition," says Burnet,‡ "landed, it might have had an ill effect on our affairs, chiefly with relation to all paper credit." Lockhart takes a

* See a letter of Lord Sunderland's in Ellis's 'Original Letters,' New Series, vol. iv. p. 249. He there says that the Ministers, by pardoning Lord Griffin, had declared before the whole world for the Prince of Wales and against the Protestant accession.

† 'Lockhart Papers,' vol. i. p. 241.

‡ 'History of his own Times,' ed. 1838, p. 826.

similar view.* Indeed we repeat that the peril of Queen Anne's Crown, at this moment, was far greater than has been generally realised. Nor is it possible to refuse sympathy to the ill-fated Chevalier de St. George—for by that name was he henceforth styled by his followers—who with a weak constitution was called on to undergo many hardships, of which not the least was sea-sickness.† After landing at Dunkirk, he courageously threw off his terrible disappointment, joined the French army, and despite partisan statements to the contrary, comported himself at the conflict of Oudenarde as became the great-great-grandson of Mary Queen of Scots, and the great-grandson of Henry the Fourth of France.‡ Moreover, while the hardships of his son Charles Edward in the '45' received due recognition from posterity, those suffered by the father at this period have been, comparatively speaking, unnoticed. Henceforth styled "Pretender" by his sister's Government, he was destined to wander over Europe without any safe resting-place. St. Germain did not suit his health,§ while the bustle and excitement of the camp seemed to relieve a monotony which induced the silent habit and almost melancholy presence which dispirited the Highlanders during the rebellion of 1715.‖

* 'Lockhart Papers,' vol. ii. p. 239.

† Macpherson's 'Original Papers,' vol. ii. p. 101.

‡ 'Memoirs of Duke of Berwick,' 1708.

§ Macpherson's 'Original Papers,' vol. ii. p. 116.

‖ 'Stuart Papers,' the property of Her Majesty, quoted in the Appendix of Lord Stanhope's 'History.'

And yet there was a playfulness about the Chevalier which accorded ill with such a character. Exceedingly attached to Marshal Villars, with whom he made the campaign of 1710 in the north of France, the Prince is described as rallying the French general as a modern Hector, and expressing a hope that M. de Torcy, the Minister of Louis the Fourteenth, was out of his "mouldy grubs;" while, when alluding to a spy from Scotland, he speaks of the *pumping* question which the detected agent of the English Government had addressed to one of his own followers. In fact he chaffed and talked slang like a modern public-school-boy.* The romance of love as well as of political misfortune coloured his youth. Although several alliances of state advantage were proposed for him, he fell enthusiastically in love with a Princess of Modena, and not until his early and happy married life with Clementina Sobieski did the former impression become entirely effaced.

His letters are interspersed with affectionate allusions to his mother, and brotherly expressions of regard for the sister who died at the age of nineteen after the small-pox, April 18, 1712. About her several interesting stories are preserved, from which we select the following. Both James Edward, and his sister the Princess Louisa, were lovers of the chase, but after a heavy fall experienced by the latter near St. Germain, her brother begged that

* Macpherson's 'Original Papers,' vol. ii. pp. 153, 155, 160. These three letters of the Chevalier's will repay perusal.

she would hunt no longer, on the ground that the sport was too rough for ladies.*

This interesting princess probably caught the small-pox when visiting, in Mary of Modena's company, the Church of the English Benedictines, where her father James the Second's remains were deposited. There was a crowd of poor people present who pressed on the royal visitors, and as the small-pox raged in Paris at the time, and the disease appeared a few weeks after, it is a natural inference that the deadly malady was contracted on this occasion.†

During this very visit to the English Benedictine Church, news was brought to Mary of Modena that peace was probable between England and France. She received the announcement with dismay, partly doubtless on the ground that her hapless son would have to leave France, and a temporary separation between the male and female members of the Stuart family ensue, although such an antagonistic view of the Treaty of Utrecht by no means tallies with the hitherto received idea that it was made to rehabilitate the Stuart cause.

The Chevalier de St. George seems to have had a better constitution than his sister Louisa, and he threw off the malady under which she succumbed, having been bled too copiously in the foot.‡

* Miss Strickland's 'Princesses of the House of Stuart,' p. 363.

† Ibid., p. 374.

‡ These details Miss Strickland derived from the nuns of Chaillot, who had been the constant associates of the exiled Royal Family. In 1711, Mary of Modena retired thither to save the expense of keeping up an

When matters of religion were at stake, the Chevalier never faltered. Although, as he said, he desired to tolerate the Church of England, he spoke thus plainly regarding his own conscience: "Plain dealing is best in all things, especially in matters of religion; and as I am resolved never to dissemble in religion, so I shall never tempt others to do it. And as well as I am satisfied of the truth of my own religion, yet I shall never look worse upon any persons, because in this they chance to differ with me; nor shall I refuse, in due time and place, to hear what they may have to say on this subject. But they must not take it ill if I use the same liberty I allow to others, to adhere to the religion which I, in my conscience, think the best; and I may reasonably expect that liberty of conscience for myself, which I deny to none." The date is May 2, 1711.*

This letter, sent to his adherents in England, probably lost him the crown; because, after all chance of converting her brother to the doctrines of the English Church had vanished, Queen Anne—as we shall show—abandoned the hopes she once presumably cherished, of leaving the crown to her nearest male relation. There is scarcely a parallel in history of similar self-abnegation; and as jesuitical advisers were ready to find balm for his sensitive

establishment at St. Germains. Chaillot had been previously known as the resort of Henrietta Maria and the Abbess of Malbuisson (see p. 112).

* Macpherson's 'Original Papers,' vol. ii. p. 225.

conscience, the merit of this unfortunate Prince becomes more worthy of record.*

Chased from France to Lorraine, and grudged even the healing waters of Plombières by his enemies, the Prince had the shrewdness never to accept the asylum offered him in Rome, because, despite his devotion to the Holy See, enemies in England might have declared that the Chevalier was under a tutelage that would admit of no tolerance towards Protestantism. He seems to have cherished a strong affection for Scotland; and when he landed at Peterhead, in 1715, no weary fugitive from the turmoil of great cities ever expressed greater delight at reaching the invigorating land-o'-cakes than did James Edward, when he joyfully exclaimed, "Thank God! I am in mine ancient kingdom."†

The Stuart Papers in Macpherson's collection afford some glimpses of the movements of the Chevalier de St. George when, France being in dire peril of invasion at the hands of Marlborough and Eugene, he bravely took his place among the defenders of his royal benefactor's realm.

Marshal Villars was a staunch Jacobite, and during his campaign in defence of Arras, in 1710, he frequently took the Chevalier with him when reconnoitring along the lines which the French had made

* The refusal of the late Count de Chambord to be restored by the Bordeaux assembly in 1871, without the white flag and the lilies of France on his escutcheon, perhaps bears some slight similitude to the conduct of the Chevalier.

† 'Stuart Papers' in Appendix of Lord Stanhope's 'History.'

for defence of the road to Paris. On one of these occasions they got into conversation with the English officers and soldiers, who told them peace was talked of when the Dutch were present, but not before Prince Eugene, and entered likewise into other general conversation. Mr. Booth—groom of the bedchamber at St. Germain—embraced the opportunity to send some Jacobite medals into the British camp, which were so popular, that thirty English officers asked for facsimiles, while several letters were addressed to the Prince's chamberlain. A trumpeter, who brought them, said that Lord Churchill * "inquired very particularly after the Chevalier de St. George." Marlborough had previously betrayed an interest in the young Prince's movements, asking one Mr. Tunstal, a Jacobite agent, why Lord Middleton was not with the Prince? and on receiving for reply an excuse on the ground of expense, answered, "One more would not augment it much." A financial policy which the Duke was apt himself to disregard in private matters.

Marshal Villars appeared to be in raptures about Sacheverell, and said he heard that people put white ribbons in their hats, and called the doctor's partisans *our* people, remarking that six thousand men formed a brave body.† Villars, thinking his policy of exciting interest for the exiled Prince had been suc-

* Id est, Marlborough. The Jacobites allowed no titles after 1688.

† Macpherson's 'Original Papers,' vol. ii. pp. 171–174. Villars had probably heard a rumour that a crowd of about this number applauded Sacheverell after his trial.

cessful, adopted similar tactics in May 1711, while waiting behind the defences he had constructed from Namur on the Meuse to the coast of Picardy. Moving from one place to another, as the tactics of Marlborough necessitated, Villars generally took the Prince with him, so that the tall, graceful figure of this would-be English King was as well known in the British camp as was his skill in horsemanship and elegance of manners, which gained admirers amongst both friends and foes.*

The Chevalier was not however with Villars in the succeeding campaign which ended so gloriously for France at Denain in July 1712. The Prince was then recovering from the small-pox, and meditating retirement into Lorraine.

There are said to have been no less than fifty-seven descendants of James the First and Charles the First, nearer in blood to the Royal Family of England and Scotland than any of the Protestant line at the time when George the First became King; † of these the family of Savoy stood nearest to that of Stuart. Victor Amadeus of Savoy had married Anna Maria, granddaughter of Charles the First, who stood next in order of inheritance to the direct descendants of James the Second. This Duke of Savoy joined the alliance against France, but he was uncertain in his after conduct, and was by no means a friend to the new order of things in England, because, a son being

* Alison's 'Marlborough,' vol. ii. p. 185.

† Macpherson's 'Original Papers,' vol. i. p. 617.

born to him, he considered that his rights were infringed by the proposed succession of the House of Brunswick.*

There was at one time some talk of an alliance between the families of Stuart and Savoy, as is shown by the following extract from Swift's 'Journal to Stella,' Letter 18, March 23, $171\frac{0}{1}$:

> "Lord Rivers told me yesterday a piece of bad news, as a secret, that the Pretender is going to be married to the Duke of Savoy's daughter. It is very bad if it be true."

Whether Swift feared the access of influence which such a marriage would give the Chevalier, or regretted that all hope of his joining the Church of England would be dissipated by his alliance with a Catholic Princess, it is difficult to say.

The Queen Dowager of England, at the time when the Brunswick succession was decided on, was Catherine of Braganza, the widow of Charles the Second, who had been espoused to him at Portsmouth in the year 1662. She finished her days at Lisbon, migrating thither at the Revolution, and enjoying a jointure of £40,000 a year, to which other sums accrued.† The Queen Dowager, a fervid Catholic, had been present in St. James's Palace when the son of James the Second was born.‡

So much concerning the minor personages of the

* See Coxe's 'Walpole,' vol. i. p. 54.

† 'Present State of the Universe,' a tract printed at the Golden Candlestick, at the Tower end of Cheapside, 1702, p. 58.

‡ Letter of Princess Anne to her sister, Dalrymple's 'Memoirs,' vol. ii. Appendix to Bk. v. p. 181.

Stuart family is necessary to make this work complete, but the course of events transfers our interest to Herrenhausen, with its trim gardens, where the Electress Sophia might be seen taking counsel with the sage Leibniz in the avenue of limes, which leads up to the palace built by the first Elector, Ernest Augustus.

CHAPTER VI.

ECHOES FROM HERRENHAUSEN.

A.D. 1688–1712.

HAVING glanced at the history of the exiled family at St. Germain, let us turn our attention from that phantom Court to a scene of more substantial dignity, with which we are more intimately concerned, namely, the home of those more fortunate cousins who dwelt on the river Leine. A central figure there was the aged Electress Sophia, a personage of such importance that it will not be amiss to consider what manner of being she was in the heyday of youth.

Mr. Kerr, a Scotch gentleman much given to travelling, who was English consul at Amsterdam, and who published in that city in the year of the English Revolution (1688) an account of his travels, gives us some insight into the Court of Hanover. "Here," he says, "I had the honour to kiss the hands of the Princess Royal, Sophia, youngest sister to the late Prince Rupert. Her Highness has the character of the Merry Debonaire, Princess of Germany, a lady of extraordinary virtue and accomplishments: she is mistress of the Italian, French, High and Low Dutch, and English languages, which she speaks to perfection. Her husband has the title of the Gentleman of Germany, a graceful and comely prince, both on foot and on horseback, civil to strangers beyond compare, infinitely kind and beneficent to people in distress, and known in the world for a valiant and experienced soldier. I had the honour to see his troops, which, without controversy, are as good men, and commanded by as expert officers, as are any in Europe. He is a gracious prince to his people, and keeps a very splendid Court, having in his stables, for the use of himself and children, fifty-two sets of coach horses. He himself is Lutheran."

The account goes on to praise Ernest Augustus' breadth of view as regards theology, because he and his children accompanied the Princess to her Calvinistic church.*

It is said that the Princess Sophia, in her youthful character of 'Merry Debonaire,' preferred the life she led in her brother Charles Louis's household at Heidelberg to the comparative seclusion of Herrenhausen.

The lofty castle overlooking the Neckar might naturally be chosen as a residence, rather than the German Versailles, which Ernest Augustus created in the suburbs of Hanover. The Princess may well have expected that her married life would be bright and cheerful, as more than one alternative alliance is

* Morriss's 'Early Hanoverians,' pp. 15, 16.

said to have been offered her, both Ferdinand, King of the Romans, and Prince Adolphus of Sweden having sought her hand.*

Hunting and the chase around Hanover, which could scarcely have presented the excitement of its English prototype, formed the chief amusement available to the household of Ernest Augustus, varied, however, occasionally by foreign travel. While his sons were serving with the army of Austria, or fighting for Venetian independence, Ernest Augustus and his wife visited Rome, and made themselves familiar with many of the Italian cities. Everywhere they were treated as if of sovereign rank, and received the respect due to the high destiny designed for them by William the Third. Ultimately, as has been previously mentioned, these titles to honour induced the Emperor to confer upon Ernest Augustus the dignity of Elector, but the proposition met with scant favour in the Electoral diet, where a majority was not forthcoming in what was called the second college. The most strenuous foes of Ernest Augustus were those of his own household, viz. the Princes of Brunswick-Wolfenbüttel, who considered their claims, as the elder branch of the house of Guelph, to be paramount, and therefore employed every artifice to prevent the election of Ernest Augustus.

On the other hand, George, Duke of Celle, the new Elector's eldest brother, supported Ernest Augustus

* Benger's 'Memoirs of Elizabeth Stuart,' vol. ii. p. 442.

loyally, so that by the influential aid of William the Third the official seal was set to the Emperor's decision, and the Elector of Hanover was represented at the conferences at Ryswick, which terminated in 1697, although he never took his seat in the College of Electors, dying at Hanover, January 23, 1698.*

In the year 1698 William the Third visited his old friend and ally, the Duke of Celle, and at the castle of Goerde he saw the widowed Electress and her son, where it is believed that future measures regarding the English succession were determined on.† But this is by no means the most important conference on the English succession between these relations and friends, because at the Loo, in King William's palace, they were again gathered together in the autumn of 1700, after the Duke of Gloucester's death had destroyed the dynastic hopes of the Protestant Stuarts.‡

In this same year, 1700, the dominions of Brunswick-Luneburg were in great danger from an attack by the Danes, so that the Elector and his uncle, the Duke of Celle, took the field, and helped to raise the siege of Tonningen, and secure the peace of Travengale.

But although the peril of invasion from the North was thus allayed, an internecine conflict was only

* Sir Andrew Halliday's 'House of Guelph,' p. 143.

† Ibid., p. 143.

‡ 'The Electress Sophia and the Hanoverian Succession,' by Prof. A. W. Ward. 'English Historical Review, vol. i. p. 485.'

averted by prompt and united action two years later, when, at the commencement of Queen Anne's reign, the aged Duke of Celle joined with his nephew, the Elector, and preserved unity in the Brunswick counsels in reference to the war about to be waged against France.

An army was suddenly marched to Brunswick and Wolfenbüttel, both of which towns were blockaded, and the recalcitrant Dukes of those provinces forced to forego their intention of joining Louis the Fourteenth.*

These Dukes were respectively named Antony Ulric and Rodolph Augustus, but as the latter led a purely literary life, all the responsibility of their pro-French policy rested with the former; but when he was obliged to desist from trying to break up the strength of Brunswick-Luneburg, no less than 40,000 men were brought into Marlborough's camp by the united family of Brunswick, Prince Ernest Augustus, afterwards Bishop of Osnaburg, and brother of George Lewis, the Elector, serving in the first campaign.

The Electress had other blood-relations whose lives are bound up with our subject, and cannot be neglected in a narrative of the Brunswick Accession. They were not all Protestants, or the Electress Sophia would not have been the legal heiress when the Act passed placing her family

* 'Some Account of the House of Brunswick.' Macpherson's 'Original Papers,' vol. i. p. 618.

next to Queen Anne in the succession, with reservations as to religion.

Two elder brothers of the Electress Sophia successively enjoyed the Palatine dignities, viz. Charles Louis and Edward.

They both professed the ancient faith of Rome, while the latter, by marriage with Anne Gonzague, Princess Palatine, a renowned devotee, had a daughter married to the Duke of Modena.* Again the Protestant heiress to Queen Anne's throne had an elder sister, Louisa, who survived until 1709, so that but for the fact that she was a Catholic, being Abbess of Malbuisson, who looked upon her Stuart cousins with unbounded devotion, she also might have claimed superior right to a place in the British Succession.

The friend of Henrietta Maria, widow of Charles the First, the Abbess, will be remembered for her able controversy with the Electress Sophia regarding the respective merits of the Catholic and Protestant faith.† The Electress found it necessary to call in

* Benedicta, Duchess of Hanover, daughter to Edward, Count Palatine, had two daughters, Charlotte Felicitas, married to the Duke of Modena, and Wilhelmina Amalia, who, having been espoused to Joseph, Emperor of Germany, was left a widow with two daughters, Mary Josephine and Mary Amelia. All these princesses were Roman Catholics, as also were the four grandchildren of Benedicta, Duchess of Hanover, who belonged to the Modenese Royal Family.—'Present State of the Universe,' printed at the Golden Candlestick, at the Tower end of Cheapside, 1702.

The Electress Sophia's eldest son Charles left a daughter married to the Duke of Orleans. This Duchess was on intimate terms with her aunt.

† The Princess Louisa had suddenly left her mother's house and embraced the Roman Catholic faith, travelling thence to Rouen, where she met her brother Edward, who conducted her to the Convent of Chaillot.

her friend Leibniz to assist her in the controversy. Two of the Princess Elizabeth's daughters had embraced a life of contemplative seclusion, the eldest, who bore her mother's name of Elizabeth, becoming so-called Abbess of the Lutheran religious retreat established at Hervorden in Westphalia. A wild and uncultivated country did not prevent distinguished philosophers from visiting the Abbess of Hervorden, the famous Descartes and William Penn, the Quaker, amongst them. She also extended her patronage to the Quietists,* who under Labbadie, had arisen in Holland about the time that Penn and Fox conducted a similar movement in the American Colonies. This daughter of the Princess Palatine exercised political power by virtue of her office as Abbess of Hervorden. She presided in a court of justice, and no less than 7000 people in and around Hervorden owned allegiance to a rule which involved membership of the German diet, to which she sent a deputy, and was required to furnish one horse and six foot soldiers when called on by the Emperor.† An apt illustration of the way in which the Imperial forces were recruited in times of need. The Act of

* The Quietists were originated by Miguel Molinos, a Spaniard, late in the 17th century. He held that religion consisted in an internal silent meditation on the merits of Christ and the mercies of God. Innocent XII., after privately discouraging, publicly condemned the doctrine in 1699, so it naturally found refuge in a Protestant retreat such as that at Hervorden. There is a curious statement in Macpherson's 'Original Papers,' vol. ii. p. 403, to the effect that the Pretender was a Quietist. Netterville, the Jesuit, hoped it might be *believed* in England.

† Benger's 'Memoirs of Elizabeth Stuart,' vol. ii. p. 448.

Succession having been passed in June 1701, it was recognized to be good policy in Hanover to receive the Earl of Macclesfield, who notified the fact at Herrenhausen, where the rejoicings were on a large scale. Fêtes illustrative of the descent of the Brunswick-Luneburg family from Henry the Second's daughter Matilda were organised, medals being at the same time struck commemorative thereof; while the fact that a Guelph married the widow of Harold, slain on Hastings field, was not left unrecorded.*

On his departure from Hanover, the Electress gave Lord Macclesfield her portrait, set in diamonds, and the Elector presented the Envoy with a massive basin and ewer of gold.†

This step in advance having been made on their behalf by adherents in England, it became necessary to frame a scheme of policy as regarded the Succession.

The individual around whose person all the affairs of Hanover seemed to centre, was the Elector's secretary, M. Robethon; and as the letters in his cabinet form the substratum of our information on this branch of our subject, we subjoin a short biogra-

* In illustration of the power and sway once held by Henry the Lion, Gibbon, in his 'Antiquities of the House of Brunswick,' Miscellaneous Works, vol. iii. p. 555, gives the following translation of the Lion's own verses:—

> "Henry the Lion is my name,
> Through all the world I spread my fame;
> For from the Elbe, unto the Rhine,
> From Hartz, unto the sea—all's mine."

† Sir A. Halliday's 'House of Guelph,' p. 146.

phical notice by the late Dr. O'Connor, librarian at Stowe when the Dukes of Buckingham owned that famous place:—

"M. Robethon was of a French refugee family. He became private secretary to King William III. and was employed by the Duke of Zell in the same capacity. He was then appointed confidential secretary to the electoral prince of Hanover, afterwards George I. This private intercourse gave him considerable ascendancy over his master; and being a man of address, great knowledge of mankind, and well acquainted with the leading members in both Houses of Parliament in England, he was enabled to act a conspicuous part. His situation with the King rendered him presumptuous and insolent. His necessities were great and his venality notorious, both Townsend and Walpole reprobating it. Consequently he became their inveterate enemy, jealously promoting the views of Sunderland. He was the most intriguing person of all the Hanoverian junto, which also comprised Count Bernsdorff, Baron Bothmar, Baron Schutz, and the Hanoverian ladies."

Dr. O'Connor, of course, states his opinion of M. Robethon as he appeared when his career was more matured than it was when he entered the Elector's service.

Another authority speaks of the Elector's secretary as follows:—

"He was a man of address, great knowledge of mankind, and well acquainted with the leading men of Parliament in England."*

As a consequence of this notoriety and familiarity with men of affairs, Robethon corresponded with the leading men in England, Holland and Hanover,

* Coxe's 'Walpole,' vol. i. p. 83.

besides having one way or the other collected holograph letters from Louis the Fourteenth, Queen Anne, Pensionary Heinsius, Marlborough, Harley, Bolingbroke, and, of course, many personal communications from his master and mistress, the Elector George Lewis and the Electress Sophia, while one or two specimens of writing by the great patron to whom he owed everything, render the collection in question doubly valuable to those who admire the character of William the Third. Taken as a whole, the famous Hanover Papers—for by that name are the contents of Robethon's cabinet known—afford indications of the characters and political ideas of the great men interested in the British Succession, such as form the best guide for a student of this thorny question—provided, that is, that he know sufficient to read between the lines when occasion requires, and do not mistake the voice of party for that of a nation, whether the writer be Whig or Tory.*

The chief Minister of the Electoral Court, after

* The Hanover Papers form part of the Stowe collection recently purchased from Lord Ashburnham by the trustees of the British Museum. They consist of a mass of correspondence ranging from 1695 to 1719, and are kept in rough leather covers, but are not yet completely catalogued. Occasionally the letters are copies of originals existing elsewhere; but very few have been printed, except those chosen by Macpherson in 1775 for his collection of 'Original Papers,' dealing with the intrigues at St. Germain and Bar-le-Duc for the purpose of restoring the elder branch of the Stuarts. Macpherson, it is true, either transcribed or translated the most valuable of the Hanover Papers, but enough remain unprinted to show their historic importance. In the second volume of his 'History of Great Britain from the Restoration to the Accession of the House of Hanover,' Macpherson also refers frequently to the Hanover Papers, and this work, too, will be found useful as a guide through this maze of hidden

1705, was Count Bernsdorff, who formerly served the old Düke of Celle in such capacity, his honoured master having passed away in that year, but in 1701 Count Platen was the Minister whom the Court chiefly consulted. Bernsdorff was celebrated for his knowledge of continental matters, and to the end of his career the Foreign Department, rather than the domestic, seems to have been his sphere: thus he was on the whole George Lewis's chief personal adviser, as regarded his relations with the Continent, although he never pretended to a knowledge of England, such as that of Bothmar. The Baron Schutz and his son filled important positions in the service of the Electress and her son, while Baron Goertz was the Minister who worked in the Tory interest.* Baron Kreyenberg, who succeeded Schutz in London, after he fell into ill-favour with Queen Anne, was also a most able agent of the Hanoverian Court, and his letters written at that period are

information. When M. de Robethon died, his son, Colonel Robethon, inherited his father's papers. Colonel Robethon, however, was a very dissipated character, and his effects were sold under an execution in 1752, when a Mr. Duane bought these volumes. He left them with his library to his relation, Mr. Michael Bray of Wimbledon, after whose decease they were purchased by Mr. Thomas Astle, who was keeper of the records in the Tower, a trustee of the British Museum, and a well-known writer on antiquarian subjects in the 'Gentleman's Magazine.' His manuscript library at Battersea Rise exceeded that of any private gentleman in England; and when he died at the age of sixty-eight, in 1803, his manuscripts and Anglo-Saxon charters were purchased, subject to certain conditions, by the Marquess of Buckingham and deposited at Stowe, where a room was fitted up in the Gothic style for their reception.—Article by Percy M. Thornton in 'English Historical Review,' vol. i. p. 756.

* Churton Collins' 'Bolingbroke,' p. 98.

full of vigour and ability. Amongst the minor members of the diplomatic corps were Schrader and Galke, who severally flitted about between London and Hanover, picking up information likely to serve their Court.

We have left to the last the man whose influence was probably felt more than that of any other member of what in after years was styled The Hanoverian Junto—we mean Baron de Bothmar. Unlike Goertz, this able diplomat—for as such he chiefly excelled—favoured the Whigs, and persuaded both Bernsdorff and his other colleagues to distrust the Tories, while he enjoined acquiescence, combined with plausible neutrality, upon the Elector and Electress. Working harmoniously with Robethon when the interests of the Brunswick-Luneburg family were at stake, this remarkable man did more to shape events than any one out of England; and when he came to that country officially, he actually chose the Prime Minister, for Lord Townsend owed his elevation to the Hanoverian Minister's good offices.

These statesmen, for in some sort, and according to their lights, they deserve the name, were continuously occupied in scheming how to retain a hold on public opinion in England, ever shifting, and dangerously prone to veer right round in matters concerning the Succession; and the contents of Robethon's cabinet tell how ably on the whole the Electoral cause was championed. Mistakes were, of course, again and again made by foreigners seeking to feel the pulse of a patient under a climatic influence, the nature of which they could not gauge. But the Brunswick cause prospered under these chosen advocates as it certainly never could have done if the principals had put themselves forward on the stage.

The year 1705 was an important epoch in the Succession question, because Robethon and Bernsdorff, those two acute diplomatists, were taken into the Electoral counsels after the old Duke of Celle's death rendered his servants free to engage their talents elsewhere, while Bothmar, established at the Hague as Hanoverian representative, saw nearly all the important documents which passed through that centre of diplomatic life, whether they were on the way to or from England. It is in the fact that much of Robethon's correspondence, together with that of Bothmar, appear in the famous Hanover Papers, that their great historic value consists.

In 1705, the year that the various territories of Hanover were united, the Electress Sophia suffered a great sorrow in the death of her daughter, the Queen of Prussia, while Whig and Tory alike appeared to compete for the honour of serving the new dynasty.

From the sources of information indicated by the various communications in Robethon's cabinet, we are enabled to present a portrait of the Electress in advancing years which may stand as a companion to the description of her early life given at the beginning of this chapter. We are in the presence of a cultured lady appreciative of literature and plilosophy, not herself a really deep student, but able intellectually to perceive Leibniz's genius, while from the exalted nature of her position she was also armed with the power to find scope for his ability, and give popularity to his name. Simple in personal tastes, most at home at Herrenhausen amongst her ducks and swans, or making the tapestry which still adorns the building, she was careful not to thrust herself or her heirs unduly before the English nation, and yet accepted the heritage they conferred on her, and desired most of all things to have inscribed on her tomb, "Sophia, Queen of Great Britain." * Some writers, on the other hand, have imputed to her undue disregard for her splendid expectations,† because when Lord Somers, in 1706, induced the Legislature to agree to the

* Coxe's 'Life of Marlborough,' chap. 59.

† There are two schools of opinion in Germany dealing with the attitude of the Electoral family towards the British Succession, one maintaining that the Electress was unduly backward in asserting her rights, while the other adduces fragmentary allusions culled from letters to agents and political friends, which are supposed to indicate a ready partizanship such as her public conduct at least belied. Herr Onno Klopp, author of the 'Fall des Hauses Stuart,' the twelfth volume of which has just been published, maintains the former, and as we think most defensible, theory, while D'O. Meinartus, in his work on the Hanoverian Succession, which saw light in 1878, takes the view that Klopp has misconstrued the Electress Sophia's politic silence, mistaking it for negligent indifference. Amongst other German writers on the subject, we find the late Dr. Schaumann and the late Professor Pauli, while the correspondence of the Electress with Leibniz affords an instructive commentary on the course of

appointment of a Regency in the event of the Queen's death, together with the naturalisation of the Electress, the latter princess treated the matter with much the same indifference with which she looked upon offers to give herself and her son a premature footing in England.*

However, when Lord Halifax, accompanied by the illustrious Addison, was despatched to Hanover with the Garter for the Electoral Prince, the Electress seems to have evinced a due comprehension of the situation.

For, first and last, neither the granddaughter of James the First, nor her heir, the Elector George Lewis, ever put their own personal claims forward,

---

events elsewhere disclosed. Historical questions of all descriptions are thoroughly threshed out by the modern Teutonic literary representatives, and there is much to be learnt from these researches by the most learned of our own inquirers. Professor A. W. Ward has recognised this to excellent purpose when elucidating the Electress Sophia's actions regarding the Succession, just as Professor Seeley, by his researches in Berlin concerning the life and times of Stein, threw a new light on the deliverance of Europe from Napoleon, telling us the story from a continental point of view. This method adopted by Professor Ward has placed the truth within the reach of those who can spare time to look into the matter ('English Historical Review,' vol. i. p. 470), for our home archives are exceedingly full of matter, and the Hanover papers themselves contain evidence undoubtedly genuine in character, affording means whereby to test other statements emanating from more doubtful sources.

It appears, however, that some copies of Robethon's letters in the Hanover collection are extant in Germany, inasmuch as Herr Klopp has several times referred to identical communications which he found amongst the Hanoverian archives, and this while most of the originals are undoubtedly in the British Museum. Of course the triumphant success of the Duke of Marlborough, when he won Blenheim, was hailed with delight at Hanover, the greatest of all soldier-diplomatists having charmed the Electress and convinced her of the reality of her prospects.

* Lord Somers to the Elector, 'Hanover Papers,' April 12, 1706.

and erred, if they erred at all, in a contrary direction. There is a very interesting minute of the Elector's in the Hanover Papers of 1704, published by Macpherson, which shows that Marlborough took the Elector George Lewis into counsel regarding his movements before Blenheim, and that the famous change of design which led to the campaign being prosecuted, not on the Meuse or Rhine, but on the Danube, was settled after discussion with the man known in history as George the First.* The year 1708 found George Lewis corresponding with Queen Anne from his head-quarters on the Rhine, having at her request accepted the command there; but although evincing an interest in all matters connected with England, he refrained from personally mixing in politics. Writing to Lord Peterborough on May 26, 1708, he says :—†

"I have adopted for a constant maxim, to take no steps concerning the affairs of Great Britain, but in concert with the Queen and with her Ministry,"—

a position as regards the Succession from which he never withdrew until events shaped themselves so as to leave the crown of England in his possession.

It was doubtless vexatious to George Lewis to find himself thwarted on the Rhine by various representatives of Southern Circles of the Empire ‡ who

* Macpherson's 'Original Papers,' vol. i. p. 690.

† 'Hanover Papers,' May, 1708.

‡ In the year 1500 Maximilian the First divided the Empire into six Circles, viz. Franconia, Bavaria, Suabia, the Rhine, Lower Saxony and

had never recognised his father's Electorate. Yet, while conducting what seemed a troublesome and uneventful campaign, the Electoral Prince reaped glory by his presence at the battle of Oudenarde, since the Guelph blood in his veins compelled him to be in the van, and sustain his family reputation for bravery. But it is obvious to a student of the military position what good service was rendered when the Rhenish provinces of Baden and the Black Forest were protected from invasion during the campaign of Oudenarde, so that Marlborough had a free hand in the Low Countries.

It was at this stage of events that a desire for peace sprang up in England, because amidst many more thoughtful men who knew how the national resources had been strained, there existed a widespread opinion that enough had been done by us to sustain the Imperial Dutch cause. The victory of Oudenarde, gained in July 1708, had not opened the road to Paris as Marlborough hoped, and the capture

---

Westphalia. In 1512 he added Austria, Burgundy, the Lower Rhine and Upper Saxony.—'State Papers,' Domestic Series, Record Office. Anne, 1705, bundle 10.

It is not generally known that George the First, during his command on the Rhine, scored a passing triumph. He detached Count Mercy in 1707 to attack General Vivans in camp near Offenburg, which was done with complete success, the enemy retiring and losing nearly a thousand men. —'Annals of the House of Hanover,' Book x. p. 531.

The French were unable to penetrate into South Germany during the time that George Lewis was general of the Imperial forces, and he handed his army over intact to the illustrious Eugene. There was a jealousy in Germany against the new Electorate of Hanover, and the Elector was not permitted to vote in the Electoral College until 1807.—Ibid., p. 535.

of Lille, Ghent, and Bruges was felt to be a result inadequate to the efforts expended.

This feeling became accentuated after the battle of Malplaquet, in 1709, when Marlborough and Prince Eugene, after a tremendous and sanguinary conflict, forced the destined saviour of France—the able Marshal Villars—off the field, and secured the investiture and fall of Mons.

But this triumph was of limited value after all, and had been bought at a fearful cost. Nothing, however, could have shaken the Whig war policy in England, had not the controversy arisen concerning Dr. Sacheverell's opinions—1709, 1710. Thereupon, however, terror regarding the Brunswick Succession seems to have seized the whole Herrenhausen *entourage*.

Many had been the devices to cause all who lived under the British flag to realise the beneficent sway prepared for them when Queen Anne should leave her throne vacant.

The States of America, for instance, were made familiar with the personal appearance of the Electress by means of portraits which were freely disseminated,* while it was even sought to instruct the heiress to

* Mr. Joseph Dudley, Governor of Boston, writes to thank her Electoral Highness for an effigies (so-called), and expresses boundless devotion.

The following letter of the late Prince George's major-domo will speak for itself, and is a fair specimen of the class which was in vogue :—

"Her Majesty in making all the rest of her subjects Easy and Happy by our late Blessed Union, has very much added to my Burden,—W^d^ to God it were yet more Heavy on Condition that every year might increase our Unanimity at Home, and our Victories Abroad. Then Madam, but not the throne in her social duties. Yet all the while an atmosphere of doubt concerning the dynastic hopes of Brunswick-Luneburg generally prevailed. Not even the effusive promises of real true men like Halifax availed to restore confidence, when astute diplomatic thinkers of Robethon's, Bernsdorff's, and Bothmar's calibre were aware, through the information given them by friends in England, that other asseverations of devotion received at Hanover from noblemen like the Duke of Buckingham and the Duke of Newcastle were untrustworthy, because these same men were sending similar assurances to St. Germain.*

The year 1709 saw Charles the Twelfth of Sweden stopped in his career of victory and left a Russian prisoner after dread Pultowa's day. For Hanover and its surroundings this event must be reckoned as savouring of a relief; for, despite the Elector's often-expressed confidence in his Northern neighbours, we now know that the tendency of Charles's mind lay in the direction of utilising such surplus power as he might obtain in restoring the House of Stuart in

yet til then will this Island be worthy to receive y[r] Illustrious House, when they will find it a Land flowing with Milk and Honey.

"Tis some time ago Madam that I took the Liberty to put into the hands of M. le Baron de Bothmar 2 or 3 Copies of my English Rules for the use of y[r] R. H. I know not whether they were ever received, but this I am sure of, that it was a very great Presumption in me to Imagine that I c[d] suggest anything in our Language which y[r] R. H. does not understand as well as,

"Madam, y[r] R. H.'s

"Most devoted and most humble servant,

"JOHN CHAMBERLAYNE."

—'Hanover Papers,' July 30, 1708.

* Macpherson's 'Original Papers,' vol. ii. pp. 41–43.

England, and so increasing his own influence in Europe.

The change of Government in England in 1712 caused the Electoral Government to prepare measures of defence against a movement which they assumed to be likely to shake the constitutional settlement upon which the Brunswick family based their hopes, and they were incited thereto by the Duke of Marlborough. Specimens of his asseverations of devotion to the Chevalier de St. George at St. Germain will necessarily be given later on. Let us now hear what he tells the Elector, Aug. 30, 1710:

"I hope there will never be found in England a considerable number of men who can be seduced to a degree capable of ruining it, by allowing themselves to be imposed upon by the artifices of Mr. Harley and others, who conduct themselves at present in a manner to leave it no longer a doubt that their views tend to bring back the *pretended* Prince of Wales."*

No wonder that when Baron Bothmar was despatched to London, he saw events too exclusively through anti-Tory spectacles.

The scene now shifts to the banks of the Thames.

* 'Hanover Papers,' August 30, 1710.

CHAPTER VII.

THE PEACE OF UTRECHT.

PROCLAIMED IN LONDON, MAY 5, 1713.

It is worthy of note that Harley on becoming practically Prime Minister, in 1710, betrayed little satisfaction, and seemed exceedingly doubtful as to the political stability of his party. As for gratitude to the frothy Sacheverell, that did not in the slightest degree influence the new Minister's conduct. We read that when Dr. Swift asked him for a living for that famous clerical agitator, Harley gave a round refusal, and showed no signs of relenting until Swift told the Treasurer the anecdote of a sailor who, during an engagement, stooped to catch a flea, and so avoided a cannon-ball, which otherwise would have taken off his head. "Then the flea shall have the living," answered Harley, recognising Swift's witty analogy between the Tory return to power by Sacheverell's aid and the above story.* But for the exercise of Swift's pen on their

* Continuation of Sir James Mackintosh's 'History,' quoting note by Sir Walter Scott in Somers' 'Tracts,' vol. xiii. p. 78. The living given to Sacheverell was that of St. Andrew's, Holborn.

behalf about this time, the Tories would not have held their ground, or made the peace of Utrecht which gained favour by means of 'The Conduct of the Allies,' a pamphlet of great ability; and indeed at one moment it looked as if Harley's popularity was waning both with the Queen and the nation; so that if he had not been incontinently stabbed by Guiscard, a refugee friend of Mr. St. John, who in a fit of desperation approached the ministerial council-table, and, unable to reach his former associate, plunged a penknife into Mr. Harley's breast, it is not improbable that the Government might have fallen to pieces. Harley was stabbed in the spring of 1711, and the public excitement against the Whigs seemed commensurate with the sudden advance of the wounded Minister's popularity. He straightway rose into high favour at Court as well as amongst the people. At the same time Lord Rochester's death left him the actual head of the Tory party.

The new Minister had borne himself with conspicuous courage, and deserved his reward, which took the form of the Premiership and an Earldom, the titles of Oxford and Mortimer being revived for him, with the addition of Baron Wigmore.

St. John also was created Viscount Bolingbroke, although, as has been before mentioned, he is said to have been dissatisfied at not receiving back an ancient Earldom which had died out in his family.

We shall enter here into no dissertation on the characters of the new Ministers, or recount in complete detail the events which led to the peace of Utrecht. It is perfectly well known that Bolingbroke, being the only Secretary of State who could speak French, was the prime mover in bringing the negotiations to an issue, while his friend Matthew Prior, the poet, first in London, and then as Ambassador in Paris, helped to conclude this much-deprecated peace. During the course of these events the Tory Ministers acted secretly, and entered into preliminaries of peace separately with France, by means of the Abbé Gaultier's intervention, while they agreed to send Lord Strafford and Robinson, Bishop of Bristol, to Utrecht for the purpose of going through what, so far as England was concerned, seems to have been a mock congress of the Powers.

Nor was this the sum total of their offending, inasmuch as the policy we are describing involved an abandonment of the brave Spanish Catalans, still in arms for their liberties, and relying on the proffered support of England.

Of course Louis the Fourteenth was thankful to come to terms with England when his resources were failing him, and the issue of a supreme struggle at or near Versailles seemed, to say the least of it, uncertain; so that the famous remark attributed to De Torcy, when he was questioned by Gaultier as to whether France wished for peace, "Ask a dying man does he wish to recover," pretty well explains the situation as it appeared to responsible statesmen in Paris.* But there was another side to the question of peace or war, considered from an English point of view, and an acute financier, whose abilities both Bolingbroke and Walpole recognised, viz. Mr. Arthur Moore—of whom we shall speak again—had formed an opinion that a nation of a little over five million inhabitants could not indefinitely support a war system with impunity, and that the strain on our national strength was likely to become perilous. But the crux of the matter really consisted in the military situation—that is, could England hope, after General Stanhope had been defeated and captured at Brihuega, December 9, 1710, to retain a hold on the Peninsula while engaging likewise in an advance towards Paris in company with the Allies? As regards Spain, a glance at the map will convince any student of the winter campaign in 1710, that the Anglo-Austrian position was one of danger, and when we know that the remaining English were deserted by the Portuguese, while Stahrenberg, the German General, had only 10,000 men against Vendôme's 20,000,† it might have been described as one almost hopeless, such as a Wellington might possibly have rendered tolerable. But then it is

* This anecdote appears in De Torcy's 'Memoirs,' but we give it here on the authority of the continuation of Sir James Mackintosh's 'History,' vol. ix. p. 265.

† Alison's 'Life of Marlborough,' vol. ii. p. 180. Stahrenberg did measure swords once with Vendôme at Villa Viciosa, but found himself obliged to retreat after a stubborn struggle.

not given to a nation to possess a Wellington and a Marlborough at one and the same time.

Out of Catalonia the Spanish nation was clearly hostile to Charles and the Germans, while it displayed an enthusiasm for Philip and the French which a student of the events that took place a century afterwards in this same country will find it hard to believe. In France, although Marlborough did take Bouchain, he was avowedly unable to advance to Paris through the network of fortifications interspersed with fortresses, which Villars, adopting Fabian tactics, threw all his genius into defending.* And under these circumstances a march to Paris was, to say the least of it, extremely problematical.

However, at this moment Marlborough's military career came to a close, and the ensuing campaign was not prosecuted by English troops, as the Duke of Ormond, the new general, had orders to remain quiescent, and obeyed them to the disgust of Germany and Holland, together, it must be owned, with the freely expressed disapproval of most right-minded people in England.

The case, however, regarding the Treaty of Utrecht stands on a different footing to the averment made that the Ministry of Lord Oxford was bent on restoring the Pretender: for while it is impossible to defend the mode of making the former, we doubt very much whether any such idea as the latter was ever adopted officially.

* Alison's 'Life of Marlborough,' vol. ii. pp. 199, 200.

Sir James Mackintosh, when meditating a history of England, dealing with events between 1688 and 1748, was permitted by Talleyrand, during the year 1814, to have free access to the diplomatic archives in Paris. He there discovered the certainty of what sundry writers, Macpherson in particular, had foreshadowed. Through the above-mentioned Abbé Gaultier, who was formerly attached to Marshal Tallard's embassy after the peace of Ryswick, Oxford carried on a secret correspondence with De Torcy, who in turn communicated some of these confidences to the Pretender.

It is the manner in which the Treaty of Utrecht was thus brought about, England and France acting secretly together (contrary to England's engagement with her allies), which has led to a general condemnation of the measures taken by Oxford and his colleagues, rendering that European settlement—whatever its general character—a by-word, recalling international intrigues of the meanest description. In the course of these dubious transactions, Oxford seems to have thrown out hints to Gaultier that he had sentiments in favour of the Pretender, but the only direct piece of evidence is in the Premier's own handwriting, when, in answer to a letter of Torcy's, he committed himself so far as to say,—

"Je parlerai à M. l'Abbé avant son départ au sujet de M. Chevalier."

This Torcy thought so much of that he sent it

gleefully to the Pretender, boasting that at last Oxford had committed himself on paper, showing that the previous communications must have been somewhat impalpable. According to Sir James Mackintosh's researches, these vague expressions of sympathy had been allowed to filter through Gaultier and Torcy, as evidencing not only Oxford's sentiments, but also those of his royal mistress, Queen Anne. The wily Minister, however, never permitted his sovereign to answer her brother's letters.

The reader can form his own ideas as to Oxford's implication in the Jacobite plots, when Queen Anne's first Minister, by turning to the 'Edinburgh Review' for October 1835, pp. 11–19, as therein is described the substance of Sir James Mackintosh's research. Beyond the reiteration of an exploded avowal of the spy Azzurini, to the effect that Bolingbroke saw the Pretender during his sojourn in Paris, when perfecting the treaty in 1712, nothing concerning that Minister's alleged complicity in Jacobite counsels is suggested until after peace had been made. True it is that Sir James Mackintosh, in one of his notebooks, has an unauthorised statement that "the first introduction of Bolingbroke into the secret negotiation was during the illness of Harley after he had been stabbed by Guiscard;" * but this surely refers to the impending treaty for peace, not, as has been inferred, to criminal intriguing against the Protestant

* 'Edinburgh Review,' Oct. 1835, pp. 19, 20.

succession. Therefore it is that the charges against Bolingbroke are relegated to a separate chapter dealing with the two last years of Queen Anne's reign.

The Hanover Papers include an interesting series of letters which passed between the Electress Sophia and Lord Strafford,* one of the plenipotentiaries sent

* Lord Strafford was a strong Tory, and as such, finding Bothmar and Schutz, the Elector's agents, taking a line purely Whiggish, reprobated a one-sided alien interference in British politics. His letters are rambling, but not the less full of good sense. The Electress, on the other hand, is both clear and concise in her statements, doubtful as to the future, and adverse to what she thought a premature peace. Thus her opinion was expressed in the following terms when first the negotiations commenced at Utrecht:—

Il me semble que l'Empereur y est asses cavallierement traité. Autre fois ce n'etoit pas par le bon plaiser du Roi de France qu'on reconnoissoit l'Empereur dans l'Empire, mais tout change dans le monde. Le dessein de la Reine etoit d'abbaisser le Roi de France, comme sa Majeste engagea tant de Princes a luis faire la guerre, et voila la France plus puissante que jamais.

Towards the close of the negotiations, on 13 Jan., 1713, Lord Strafford wrote to the Electress: "The minister of the four circles of the Empire has been with us, and has given us a memorial for the Queen complaining how ill they should be left without Strasburg. They were answered that their not having that town was to be attributed only to the fault of the Princes of the Empire, who none of them found their contingents but hired their troops to serve in Flanders, and when a proposition was made for a general cessation, which the allies being united might have obtained that place, they opposed it, and for the sake of Prince Eugene would follow chimerical projects of new battles and sieges."

As for the state of public opinion in England after the peace was concluded, Lord Strafford writes to the Electress from the Hague on 24 July, 1713: "Bless God I am born an Englishman, in spite of all our feuds and divisions, which as long as it does not come to a civil war is only a preservative of our libertys. I believe it is pretty plain now we peacemakers shant be hanged at our return as we were threatened. For daily our countrymen grow more and more pleased with the peace. And how have we been made the dupes of others to pay their war."

by England to the Congress at Utrecht; and although we now are aware that the English representatives were merely acting, arguing, that is, over matters settled privately between France and themselves, yet the matter contained in these above-named documents is not to be disregarded.

The value of Strasburg for purposes of offence was speedily demonstrated, for in the succeeding duel between Eugene and Villars after Denain in July, 1712, the latter general passed the Rhine and raided through the Black Forest to Freiburg, using the Alsatian fortress as his base of operations. We read of Germany suffering at this time from lack of that unity which the efforts of Stein and Bismarck gained for her in later years. And indeed Lord Strafford had gauged the strength of semi-exhausted France and Austria better than most of his contemporaries, for he told the Electress that the Emperor would very likely suffer defeat and be in danger of an Hungarian revolt. This prediction was realised when Italy became hostile to the Imperialists, who, conscious of their danger, made peace at Rastadt on March 6, 1714.*

Lord Strafford's letters are enlivened by pictures of incidents which occurred in the quaint town of Utrecht during the congress, and he tells us of

* A summary by the author compiled from the 'Hanover Papers,' which deals with the peace of Utrecht, appears in the 'English Historical Review,' vol. i. p. 765. According to Alison's 'Marlborough,' vol. ii. p. 233, Austria succumbed on this occasion because her resources failed her.

the *pleureuses*, or weepers, worn by the French, who appeared in mourning for the Dauphin and Dauphiness of France, and their child, cut off by a mysterious disease, which raged in Europe. Truly the position of Louis the Fourteenth was lamentable alike socially and politically.

In his childless old age he was destined to see his dearly bought conquests shrink, and his country reel under poverty's fell grasp, while not even the mercy shown him by the Peace of Utrecht could refill the public coffers or render the suffering people content. Lastly, and to his credit he felt the vexation sorely, Louis was constrained to abandon James the Second's unfortunate son, who was henceforth destined to become a desperate vagrant, forced by the very necessities of his birth and present condition to scheme on to the end.

The territorial changes made by the Treaty of Utrecht powerfully affected the European system, and created a condition of things which, in spite of several wars, was not seriously altered until the revolutionary struggle occurred, which closed the 18th century.

Disparage it as you will, the Treaty of Utrecht contained a guarantee for the Protestant succession in England, and so claims something more than passing mention here. As viewed by contemporary observers, and as commented on by historians who dwelt comparatively near to the events of 1710–13, the action of the Oxford Ministry has been judged so completely from the standpoints of Whig and Tory, that, despite Macaulay's essay, the abovementioned hard fact has not been duly recognised.

Those who have even followed the sparse outline of the preceding pages will know that the statesmanship in vogue in Queen Anne's time was, for the most part, of a crooked order. We have cited noble exceptions, of which Somers is the leading example; but the fact remains, and when we know that Harley and St. John gained their power by intrigue, it is scarcely to be wondered that they strove to hold it by the same unworthy tactics.

But what we most desire to impress on our readers is this: if peace was attainable at all in 1710 and 1711, the only certain means to hand were those adopted by the Tory Government, who, having supplanted the Marlborough family in the Queen's graces, were then called on to cut the ground finally from under the feet of those brilliant favourites, supported as they were to the last by all the influence and ability of the Whig junto, comprising Somers, Cowper, Halifax, Sunderland, and Walpole.

Nor should it be forgotten that any peace with France which contained an acknowledgment of the Protestant succession in England—and none other was possible—had necessarily to be negotiated for with those who were conducting one of the greatest wars Europe had ever seen, in order to replace James the Second's son on the English throne. The problem seemed insoluble, and that it ever received a passing solution is, we fear, due to the fact that methods were used such as men of the late Lord Stanhope's type have generally deprecated.

So far as British interests were concerned, they were not uncared for by the high contracting parties who represented us on this occasion; and although even in this particular there was much to deplore, the diplomatic instrument which gained Gibraltar, and for the moment thrust back France on the American frontier of Canada, is not one which, read by the light of later events, Englishmen should entirely condemn.

Lord Bolingbroke, when as Mr. St. John he came into office in 1710, had striven to seize on Quebec by means of a joint naval and military expedition sent out on the suggestion of Colonel Nicholson, who received his inspiration from some Indian chiefs hostile to the French.

Escorted by twelve men-of-war, this fleet consisted of six store ships and a number of transports, which arrived at Boston on June 4, 1711, but found the authorities unprepared to furnish the necessary provisions, so that the troops had to be landed, and encamped for a time. This delay probably ruined the venture, for Admiral Sir Hovenden Walker had his fleet dispersed in a violent north-east gale, and getting amongst the northern rocks and shoals, lost eight transports with 900 soldiers and seamen on board, whereupon he desisted from the attempt to reach Quebec;* so that the Government might regard themselves as favoured by fortune when at Utrecht they secured fishing rights and the sovereignty generally of Hudson's Bay, Nova Scotia, and Newfoundland.†

The chief articles of this famous treaty were the acknowledgment of the Queen's title and the Protestant succession by France; the removal of the Pretender from the French dominions; the renunciation of the crown of Spain by the Dukes of Berri and Orleans, the contingent succession of that crown being secured to the Duke of Savoy; the abovementioned cessions in Canada, which, besides Hudson's Bay and Newfoundland, included Nova Scotia. The possession of Gibraltar and Minorca secured to England; the demolition of Dunkirk guaranteed; barriers respectively retained for the States, the Emperor, and the Duke of Savoy, on the sides of Flanders, the Rhine and the Alps. The restoration of Lille, Aire, Bethune, and St. Venant to France, the articles concerning these hardly-won fortresses causing grave discontent; the cession of Sicily to the Duke of Savoy, and the proffered cession of Naples, Milan, Sardinia, and the Spanish Nether-

* Wynne's 'British Empire in America,' 1770, vol. i. p. 144.
† Harrop's 'Bolingbroke,' p. 148.

lands to the Empire, most of which territory afterwards accrued to the house of Hapsburg.*

It is, however, not with the influence of these territorial changes on Europe that we are here concerned so much as with the circumstances that preceded the signature of a treaty said to have been designed in direct antagonism to the Brunswick expectations of succeeding to the English throne, but which issued in such a shape as to become the very sheet-anchor of their dynastic hopes, and a security for the perpetuity of their realisation.

It should, however, be added that the commercial clauses of the treaty, which were designed by Mr. Arthur Moore—a man beginning life as a footman, who had gradually raised himself by industry—were rejected ignominiously by Parliament, although they contained, according to the opinion of the best judges, the seeds of a fiscal system such as the younger Pitt favoured, and which in after times of European tranquillity was formulated by Adam Smith, and blossomed into life under Peel, Cobden, and Gladstone.

Mr. Moore was exercising a strong influence over Bolingbroke at the time of the Peace of Utrecht, and lived to hold a kindred power over Sir Robert Walpole. This remarkable man, Mr. Arthur Moore, had thought out the principles upon which the wealth of a people depends, and it is to Bolingbroke's credit

* We owe this succinct synopsis to the continuation of Sir James Mackintosh's 'History,' p. 285.

that he too saw the benefit of extended commerce between the nations.*

Regarded, then, from the point of view of an adherent of the Brunswick family, the Peace of Utrecht was not the inimical treaty that has been believed. Yet the fact that better terms might have been obtained at Gertruydenberg in the spring of 1710 has led men of thought and honour to condemn the settlement of 1713; † while so overjoyed was Louis the Fourteenth at the signing of this peace, that, through Lord Bolingbroke, he sent Queen Anne six splendid dresses, and two thousand five hundred bottles of champagne.‡

It should not be forgotten that in after years Bolingbroke himself admitted in his letter to Sir William Wyndham, that France was treated too leniently on this occasion. On the other hand, a nation of little more than five millions, whose population was believed to have decreased in the last ten years, stood saddled with a debt of fifty-four millions, more than thirty-seven millions of which had been added during Anne's reign, and which bid fair to become larger still if an end had not been put to this system of perpetual warfare.§ Again, to believe that France, with her native wealth and resources,

* For adequate recognition of Mr Arthur Moore's talents see Harrop's 'Bolingbroke,' p. 149.

† The late Lord Stanhope is persistently hostile to the Peace of Utrecht.

‡ Alison's 'Marlborough,' quoting Capefigue, vol. ii. p. 219.

§ Alison's 'History of Europe,' vol. iv. p. 538, Revenue Tables.

would have long submitted to a shameful peace, whereby territory and money were ruthlessly wrenched from her at the gates of Versailles, is to ignore all the teachings of history past and present. Sir Robert Walpole could not have nurtured England's resources unless he had taken the Peace of Utrecht as the corner-stone of his policy.

We may cite the Duke of Marlborough as being conscious of the desirability that a peace should be speedily made, although he doubtless hoped so to crush Marshal Villars as to find his way straightway to Paris. He writes to Bolingbroke from the siege of Bouchain on August 20, 1711, as follows:—

> "The siege so far as it depends on me shall be pushed on with every vigour, and I do not altogether despair but that, from the success of this campaign, we may hear of some advances made towards that which we so much desire. And I shall esteem it much the happiest part of my life if I can be instrumental in putting a good end to the war, which grows so burdensome to our country, as well as to our allies." *

The Pretender, on the other hand, regarded the approaching signature of this peace with something akin to despair, dreading the possibility of being driven into some Swiss or Papal refuge which he could not leave without passports, and he foresaw that his political effacement would thereby be accomplished.† Vainly did he strive to provide guarantees against such eventualities, and although the Jesuit Plunket flitted in and about Utrecht during the

* Coxe's 'Marlborough,' vol. vi. p. 92.

† Macpherson's 'Original Papers,' vol. ii. p. 294.

diplomatic gatherings which took place at the Bishop of Bristol's house, yet the chief features of the treaty remained fixed which banished the son of James the Second from France.

Pending the outcome of these deliberations, both James Edward and his sister were seized with the attack of small-pox, which has been previously mentioned as having carried the good princess from the reach of all the troubles environing her and hers.

On recovery from his illness, the Pretender, under the safe conduct of the Emperor, obtained a refuge in Bar-le-Duc, in the Duke of Lorraine's dominions, that sovereign resolutely refusing to eject his guest when the demand for such action became pressing on the part of England.

There has been no attempt made here to give an exhaustive account either of the way in which this famous European settlement came into being, or of the scope and design which characterised its clauses, but we have striven simply to show what influence the Treaty of Utrecht exercised on the Succession question in England. And from this aspect the family of Brunswick-Luneburg has every reason to rejoice at the conclusion of peace in 1713. But a potent foe has lately urged with all the prestige that possession of the historic faculty can confer, that the seeds of evil were left rooted in the soil of Spain, when by virtue of the Peace of Utrecht a Bourbon sovereign stood triumphant, if harmless for immediate purposes of aggression at Madrid.

From the omission to force Philip from the throne of Spain, he traces the mysterious family compact of 1733, which, carried to its logical conclusion, and faithfully adhered to for at least a century, threatened the peace of Europe constantly, and broke it more than once.* And in so far as five years alone sufficed to prove what hidden power lurked in that inert mass which made up the ancient Spanish kingdom, this part of the case, at least, is proven against those who disregarded Spain as played out when they left a Bourbon on her throne. But, on the other hand, Alberoni himself could not have persuaded the Spanish people to let him weld together their resources on behalf of a cause in which their sympathies were not enlisted.

No writer has ever more eloquently described the righteous enthusiasm begotten of the great principle of nationalities as applied to occasions when whole races of men have elected to leave their homes and die for the sake of the race from which they sprung, than Professor Seeley. No historian has more clearly perceived that the stirring up of such sentiment in 1808–9 proved a beacon light whereby the deliverers of Europe from Napoleon saw their way to effect a necessary salvation for their suffering people; but if, on the other hand, he considers that the statesmen who concluded peace at Utrecht in 1713 ought to have withheld their pens from the

* 'The House of Bourbon,' by Professor J. R. Seeley, 'English Historical Review,' vol. i. p. 86.

parchment until Spain was subjugated and lay bleeding at the feet of Charles, then we say that this nineteenth-century teacher has deserted his flag, and denied to the peasants of Castile and Leon that which he granted willingly to their descendants, namely, the right to choose their own rulers.

It has been shown, however, which is enough for the limits of this work, that there was neither let nor hindrance to the Brunswick succession in a single line of the Utrecht treaty. Let us then turn towards England at this moment, and endeavour to discover the views of Queen Anne.

CHAPTER VIII.

QUEEN ANNE AND HER EXILED BROTHER.

In dealing with early eighteenth-century politics in England, some speculation is inevitable regarding the last Stuart Queen's desire to see her brother named in the succession, rather than that branch of her house settled in Germany whose representatives claimed descent from James the First's daughter Elizabeth. In the present summary it is proposed to place speculative theory in the background, and adduce several facts for the reader's information, and so arm him to arrive at his own conclusion.

It is well known that the Princess Anne was originally one of those who doubted whether Mary of Modena was really the mother, or James the Second the father, of the Chevalier de St. George; and if there is one argument stronger than another which has helped to dissipate that strange error, we find it in the fact that when her sister and children were dead, Queen Anne turned instinctively towards the nearest blood-relation she possessed.

After the death of her husband in 1708, this sentiment became necessarily more keen, and it is to the Queen's credit that she kept her natural feelings in strict subordination to considerations of public duty both in sustaining the Church of England, and in acting according to parliamentary authority. Nearly all the indications of this brotherly affection which have filtered out bear reference to the period when, in her widowhood, James the Second's daughter was left almost desolate. Under these circumstances it was natural that the Queen should from time to time have held converse with distant cadets of her own family, such as Sheffield, Duke of Buckingham, who had married James the Second's natural daughter, Catherine Darnley, while she frequently gave her confidence to those who had known or served her father.

There is a passage in the 'Lockhart Papers,' vol. i. p. 317, which has been much commented on, and it certainly proves that the Duke of Hamilton—an acknowledged advocate of the Jacobite succession—was also on terms of intimacy with Queen Anne, who took counsel with him regarding this thorny subject.

After Dr. Sacheverell's trial, and just before Godolphin's Government fell, Mr. Lockhart had obtained an address from the barons and freeholders of Edinburgh, calling on Parliament to allow the sovereign free choice of her own servants. The Whig Ministry had endeavoured to get the Queen's favourite, Mrs. Masham, dismissed, in order that the Duchess of Marlborough might resume her former influence at Court. Highly resenting this interference with her private affairs, the Queen had declared how strongly she desired to be secured against such attempts in future. Therefore it was that when Mr. Lockhart—Jacobite though he was well known to be—appeared with his scroll at Court, the Duke of Hamilton being present, he received a gracious answer to the address inscribed thereon, and was told in so many words by the Queen that although he had almost always opposed her measures, she did not doubt of his affection to her person, and hoped he would not concur in the design against Mrs. Masham, or for bringing over the Prince of Hanover. Of course the latter allusion was to the proposal that the Electoral Prince should reside in England, which had been brought forward by the Tory Lord Haversham, and cannot be interpreted as implying any general enmity on the Queen's part to the Brunswick Succession. Lockhart, however, endeavouring to improve the occasion, averred that, as regards Hanover, Her Majesty might judge from the address he presented, that "the bringing over any of that family, either now or any time hereafter," would not be acceptable to the Scotch constituency which the bearer represented.

Of course Lockhart's shaft was directed against the Brunswick-Luneburg claims in particular, and it certainly is a portentous circumstance, if true, that the Queen, after smiling on Lockhart, should have said to the Duke of Hamilton, she believed the Jacobite member to be an honest man and a fair dealer, and that the Duke replied, "he could assure her Lockhart liked her Majesty and *all her father's bairns*."

But as this story rests on the *ipse dixit* of his Grace, the moment has arrived for testing this evidence by the light afforded in such of the Hamilton papers as have been disclosed to the public.

Now, a letter was written by the Duke of Hamilton, in January, 1712, to Lord Middleton, James Edward's political adviser, which certainly does show the state of the Queen's mind at that period. After averring that she considered the crown as a trust for which she was accountable, and acknowledging that the Prince's misfortunes had affected her deeply, she nevertheless lamented that they had been brought upon him "by imbibing tenets repugnant to her people."

So far the Queen; but the Duke, whose death was so heavy a blow to the Jacobites, concludes as follows:—

"The country will never receive a King from France, nor will the English suffer themselves to be governed by a Roman Catholic. I would rejoice to see the Prince one day restored, but I declare against having any concern in civil wars. To be plain, you should lose no time in taking him away from France, and not wait until you be compelled by a public or private article in the treaty (that of Utrecht then pending).

"Go with him to a Protestant country, and marry him, as soon as possible, to a Protestant.

"I wish you were safe in Sweden." *

* Hamilton's 'Transactions,' p. 245.

These words seem to take the sting out of a generally credited assertion which attributes sinister intentions to the Duke of Hamilton when in 1712, just before his death in a duel in Hyde Park with Lord Mohun, he was chosen to be Queen Anne's Ambassador at Paris. He would clearly have sanctioned no attack on the Protestant Succession. He was stabbed (accidentally, as the Whigs contended) by General Macartney, Lord Mohun's second, and his secret instructions have never been revealed.

Now the source from which the above-cited extract is derived is not likely to enable us to arrive at the exact truth without due consideration of the circumstances under which the author of Hamilton's 'Transactions' gained his information, and due allowance for the fact that he wrote as a bitter traducer of the great Duke of Marlborough. Party writing is at all times to be scanned with caution, and the late Dr. Hill Burton has perceived the consequent untrustworthiness of this work as an historical guide. But, on the other hand, not only was the compiler of the 'Transactions' connected with the Hamiltons, but he certainly had obtained access to some of their family archives. Moreover, the above-quoted sentences bear the impress of genuineness, and therefore seem available for historical purposes. If then, as seems probable, Queen Anne held these decided views as to the impossibility of her brother succeeding unless he became a Protestant, all her expressions of sisterly sympathy with that unfortunate Prince must be read in the light of such sentiments with regard to the Succession. On the other hand, the doubts and anxieties of Robethon, Bothmar, Schutz, and the other Hanoverian agents, are to some degree justified, although it is still open to question whether they used the wisest means to guard against the dangers of the situation.

A more implicatory document has been brought prominently forward, on Miss Strickland's authority, and is said to have been found by that authoress in the collection of State papers in Paris, and the reference given is "2—Collections. Bib. du Roi;' the researches in question having been made during the Orleanist *régime*.

The extract in question from an assumed letter to Louis the Fourteenth from Queen Anne, must have been written after the Peace of Utrecht had been signed. It runs as follows:—

> "I have done all that is possible in the present juncture in favour of a Prince whose interests are sustained by your generosity.
>
> "I doubt not that he will be fully convinced of this himself, and that all the world will agree in the same.
>
> "I repeat yet, Monsieur my brother, that the consideration of your friendship will be a motive very effective to engage me for the future in his interests, and in those of his family."

Now this communication, read by the light of our previous knowledge, comes to this. The Queen had privately expressed her views regarding her brother, and signified her own possible acquiescence in his taking the headship of the family, provided that religious scruples did not hinder him from acquiescing in the conditions preliminary to any possible change in the Succession. Whether Queen Anne wished it or not, the Electress Sophia remained the legal heir so long as James Edward preserved his unbending attitude of devotion to the Roman Church. Hence the conclusion of the Queen's letter does not really bear the significance which at first seems to be attached to it. The peace between France and England was regarded as being precious to both countries, while the real interests of James Edward's family were certainly not bound up in pressing on a civil war in England. Indeed the events of 1715 and 1745 prove such an interpretation of the Queen's desires for her kinsman to be founded on the truth.

The extract from M. de Torcy's memoirs, founded on the then Lord Jersey's assurances, may be similarly disposed of :—

> " Scavez vous bien que Madame Prothose (la Reine Anne) a des sentiments fort tendres pour M. de Montgoulin (le Roi d'Angleterre)," *

while at the same time it shows reason for the impression which the Chevalier retained to the last, that his sister desired to restore him, the truth being distorted by flatterers, and hidden by interested adherents; and indeed the words, " if the Princess dies I am lost," † concur with the spirit that did James Edward so much harm, when, after George

* 'Edinburgh Review' on Cooke's 'Bolingbroke,' Oct. 1835.

† Coxe's MSS. in British Museum, vol. 51, folio 1.

the First came to the British throne, he issued a declaration mentioning the good intentions of his sister towards him.* With this explanation our readers will not, however, interpret Queen Anne's views as regards the Succession incorrectly; and the further statements of the Queen made to Sheffield, Duke of Buckingham, to Archbishop Dawes and others, will appear in their true aspect as soon as the subject is fully discussed. In the Stuart papers, now in the Royal library at Windsor, the following opening sentence occurs in a letter of the Duke of Berwick to his half-brother, the Pretender :—

> "St. Germains, April 20, 1714.
>
> "M. Orbec (Ormond) has at last spoken plain to Mr. Albert (Anne), and they are both agreed to bestir themselves in behalf of M. Raucourt (James)."†

This announcement means very little, for Ormond's wish was doubtless father to the thought, and ever sanguine in interpreting the signs of his times, his career was fruitful in failures begotten of schemes ill-digested and not carried to a conclusion. That the Queen's personal sympathies were at St. Germain rather than at Herrenhausen no one can doubt, but having an inkling of this fact the Jacobites magnified every hopeful circumstance, and interpreted goodwill and civility into partisanship, which foreboded arbitrary interference with the law. That

* Smollet's 'History of England,' vol. ii., p. 278.

† Lord Stanhope's 'History of England from the Peace of Utrecht,' vol. i., Appendix, p. 8.

Queen Anne ever gave Ormond the assurance mentioned in April, 1714, is contrary to a mass of evidence which demonstrates that then she had surrendered all hope of seeing her brother placed in the position his birth entitled him to but for his father's conduct in bringing his son up a Catholic, and riding roughshod over English liberties. Doubtless the sacrifice was considerable which Anne was forced to make, for she knew but little of her cousins of Brunswick-Luneburg, nor had affection for her father's memory ever been absent from her thoughts. It is said that he penned an affecting letter to the Princess Anne just before his death, while Mary of Modena had written to her another document of like character, conveying his last blessing and forgiveness, praying that God might convert her heart and confirm her in the resolution to repair to his son the wrongs done to himself.* Truly the Queen was left in a painful situation, and might be forgiven if she did lend an ear to the voices of those friends to her dynasty and family who, nevertheless, failed to see the immensity of that principle at stake when a choice had to be made between a representative of Rome or one from the land of Luther. Queen Anne gauged this, despite the doubting heart which beat in a sister's breast, and generations yet unborn will bless her memory for so deciding.

* See Prof. A. W. Ward's article on Anne, 'Dictionary of National Biography,' vol. i. p. 451.

Convincing evidence will be given, we believe, that towards the close of Lord Oxford's rule the Queen stood as staunch to the Brunswick Succession as anybody in the land. It is fortunately open to loyal Englishmen to indulge natural sympathy for the interesting Stuart family in the hard lot which awaited them at this period, and this because the last of their line, Henry, Cardinal of York, made the clearest avowal within his power, that upon the family of Brunswick-Luneburg, and on no other, had the mantle of the ancient line of Stuart fallen. It is written in quarters where no negative reply can, from the nature of the case, receive a hearing, that the sins of the fathers are visited on the children, but if ever human pity deservedly welled up and endowed misfortune with a romance such as time will never dim, it has been in the case of James Edward Stuart.

Having discussed his half-sister's natural preference for him, let us turn for an instant to the letters which he is known to have written to the English Queen. They are the work of a clear writer, endowed with a natural style; and the feelings gracefully expressed therein appeal to all who peruse them with native eloquence, to which the enforced silence of his sister stands in remarkable contrast. For instance, on March 28, 1712, shortly before the Duke of Hamilton was to start as Ambassador to Paris, the Chevalier wrote in his own hand as follows:—

"In the present situation of affairs, it is impossible for me, dear sister, to be any longer silent, and not to put you in mind of the honour and preservation of your family; and to assure you, at the same time, of my eternal acknowledgment and gratitude, if you use your most efficacious endeavours towards both. Give me leave to say that your own good nature makes me already promise it to myself, and with that persuasion, I shall always be ready to agree to whatever you shall think most convenient for my interest, which, after all, is inseparable from yours; being fully resolved to make use of no other means but those you judge most conclusive to our mutual happiness, and to the general welfare of our country.

"Your most entirely affectionate brother." *

In another more extended and less telling communication, the Chevalier pleads his right for prior consideration to the distant cousins at Hanover, of whom, nevertheless, he speaks as kinsmen, and in kindly terms. It requires no vivid imagination to conceive the heart-searchings which necessarily assailed the English Queen when these letters were placed before her, the wily Oxford being doubtless in full cognisance of their existence, and resolved to prevent his mistress sending any letter of message to her brother.

The desolation which accompanies a childless middle life necessarily becomes more pronounced when the memory of happier hours is ever present to the mind. Anne, when Princess of Denmark, lived in Wandsworth with her husband during James the Second's reign, and in 1684 lost her first child, five others, including the Duke of Gloucester,

* Macpherson's 'Original Papers,' vol. ii. p. 295.

following them to the grave; since which bereavements she had seen her dethroned father committed to a foreign grave; while, to crown all, her husband had been taken from her by death.*

Her sister Mary also lay by her great husband in Westminster Abbey. Under these circumstances the yearnings of her heart for family affection could alone be satisfied by turning to its male representative. This yearning could be freely indulged if she could induce him to forsake a religion she deemed that no English monarch could profess without peril to good government and to national welfare.

Between James Edward and the Succession there was an impenetrable gulf fixed, yet Queen Anne did not, until towards the close of her life, gauge the situation in all its intensity. The Chevalier had been taught to believe "that the Tory party in England wanted him as much as he wanted them." †

It was not so in fact, and any dispassionate student of the life at St. Germain—which, so far as Mary of Modena and the female part of her family was concerned, alternated with retreats to the convent of Chaillot—must come to the conclusion that it was well for England, and probably for the Stuarts themselves, that the experiment of a Restoration never was tried. Sooner or later, in Lord Bolingbroke's

* Queen Anne's hostility to the Godolphin *régime*, and to Lord Somers in particular, was partly owing to the desire evinced by the latter to drive Prince George of Denmark from the Admiralty.

† Bolingbroke's 'Letter to Sir William Wyndham,' p. 276.

opinion, "the Court of St. James would be constituted, if ever he (the Pretender) was restored, in the same manner as that of St. Germain."*

Therefore it seems to have been happily decided by Providence that the surviving brother and sister of the ancient Stuart line never met in Queen Anne's last years, or her family tenacity, strengthened by the personal charm of the brother she pitied so deeply, might have led to the temporary setting aside of principles on which England's greatness depended and still depends.

Queen Anne will be now remembered in history as having foregone the claims of race, preferring those of religion and constitutional law such as Englishmen had deliberately resolved should obtain in this little island.

From the miscellaneous and undated papers at the Record Office, the two following documents, which we found, have been selected as likely to be unfamiliar, and to make an interesting conclusion to the chapter devoted to Queen Anne.

The first gives us a vivid picture of Her Majesty's journey to *the* Bath—to use a stock phrase of the time—for cure of her oft-recurring ailment, the gout.

Her Majesty drove to Reading amidst an escort of Horse Guards and Grenadiers. Half-a-mile from the town troops *resident* in the place received her, and accompanied the Royal *cortège* to Newbury, where

* Bolingbroke's 'Letter to Sir William Wyndham,' p. 176.

the local regiment succeeded; the same change of escort being observed at Hungerford and Marlborough; while at Sandy Lane, a detachment from Devizes undertook to guard the Queen until she reached her destination.* The people on the route were assembled to welcome their Queen with true British loyalty. Rather a contrast, this, to a Royal journey in our own times, when the smoke and hurry of a railway journey are substituted for the drive through scattered market-towns and pleasant country lanes.

Secondly, we transcribed the following draft, in Queen Anne's own hand, of a speech, which is clearly intended to supply arguments in favour of Lord Oxford's Ministry when they brought about the Peace of Utrecht, and may be considered to present the real sentiments of its Royal author.

> "The best way of preserving the religious and civil rights and of serving the Protestant Succession, as well as the best proof which they can give of their real concern for it, is to proceed with unanimity and temper in supplying the necessary occasions of the government, and in establishing Peace at home by discountenancing the restless endeavours of those factious spirits who attempt to sow jealousies, and to raise groundless fears in the minds of her Majesty's people." †

---

* Record Office, Domestic Series. Anne, bundle 30.

† Ibid.

CHAPTER IX.

THE DESIGNS OF LORD BOLINGBROKE.

A.D. 1713–14.

HENRY ST. JOHN, Viscount Bolingbroke, was the best speaker and one of the most remarkable writers of his time. His youth not being steadied by the ballast which every man of genius needs, he pursued during the prime of life an unfortunate course of profligacy, and later in his dazzling career, injured his reputation by propounding crude ideas on theology.

But for the marvellously attractive style in which he clothed these wild sallies of a darkened heart, few readers would ever have stopped to scan pages, to which the widest latitudinarian of the nineteenth century never dreams of appealing as records of sound philosophy.

In spite of these shortcomings, Henry St. John succeeded in charming those into whose society he was thrown. Not only was his bearing noble and worthy his origin—for he came of an ancient family long settled at Battersea—but God had endowed him with a manly presence such as put mere good looks into the shade. Such remarkable graces of person allied to rare wit and eloquence reconciled men and women to the incongruities of his character. The kind of influence which Lord Bolingbroke exercised over his contemporaries is illustrated by the great Duke of Marlborough's declaration, made when grieving over the loss of his only son, Lord Blandford, that "he loved Henry St. John as a son." Nor should this friendship between the soldier-diplomatist and Queen Anne's Secretary of State be lost sight of when striving to unravel the tangled history of this period.

Again, the fascination exercised over later statesmen and students of history by the magic of his literary style and the brilliance of his statecraft, might be shown by many examples. Lord Chatham instanced his style as worthy of imitation, and submitted the attainted nobleman's political writings to his son, William Pitt, the peerless Minister of George the Third, who never ceased to lament the loss of Lord Bolingbroke's speeches, believed to be superior to his written utterances, which were themselves on a level with the finished compositions of Addison and Swift.

Such was the man who, nominally a subordinate to Lord Oxford, yet by sheer force of ability became the main wheel of that machine which carried on the government between 1710–14. He was believed by his contemporaries to cherish a desire to restore the ancient Stuart line of Kings without the guarantee which was considered to be indispensable, if the constitutional liberties handed down from our fathers were to be preserved. Now it has been already indicated how far the Earl of Oxford was implicated in a conspiracy to restore James Edward, by the light of those researches which Sir James Mackintosh pursued in Paris during the allied occupation of 1814, and it is here proposed to discuss the evidence then collected, which, according to hostile writers, involves Bolingbroke in a preconceived conspiracy to strangle the constitution, and render solemn parliamentary decisions regarding the Succession null and void.

Putting aside certain asseverations of the Jacobite spy Azzurini, who declared that Lord Bolingbroke had two interviews with the Pretender at Paris during 1712—a statement which has been proved to be based on misapprehension—the counsel for the prosecution* takes timely refuge in the conversations held by the British Minister with D'Iberville, the French chargé d'affaires in London during 1713, when the Duc d'Aumont took his departure from England. What is the sum and substance of this alleged criminality as set forth in an elaborate indictment, framed in such a way as to be a pithy echo of the State prosecution preserved in the national archives? Why, this, and this alone. A crisis was believed to be at hand after the Queen had been prostrated by an attack of illness, and D'Iberville relates to Louis the Fourteenth an ac-

* 'Edinburgh Review,' Oct. 1835, p. 20.

count of his conversation with the British Secretary of State. The Pretender, said the latter, had no chance of success, " tant qu'il sera Catholique, pas même en epousant une ' princesse Protestante.' " He did not blame the impatience of the Jacobites, " mais, dit-il, nous connoissons mieux qu'eux la difficulté qu'il y a de manager les differens esprits dont le Parlement est composé. Il faut pour cela plus." *

The very echo this of that manifest drift of opinion in England which secured the throne to the Brunswick-Luneburg family.

So we must seek further afield for the evidence which is to fix treason on Bolingbroke prior to his departure from England after George the First assumed the crown. In the latter years of Lord Oxford's administration, he seems to have left to his eloquent colleague the task of attracting doubters to the Tory party, satisfying alike the scruples of Jacobites eager to see the ancient faith restored with the legitimate King, as well as those who desired to take security that mass should not be said at St. Paul's by Royal authority.

There is a very good illustration of Lord Bolingbroke's difficulties and of his method in dealing with Jacobite malcontents, in the 'Lockhart Papers.' †

The Government had issued their famous proclamation against the Pretender, which offered £5000 for his person, dead or alive, if he landed in England —a ministerial action which literally struck the

* 'Edinburgh Review,' Oct. 1835, p. 20. † Vol. i. p. 476.

Jacobites dumb with amazement, because the House of Commons, at Oxford's and Bolingbroke's instigation, had just refused the back pay of the Hanoverian contingent which had followed Prince Eugene rather than remain inactive with Ormond, when the British Government enjoined no further military operations on their General.

This refusal had been held to imply disregard of the Brunswick-Luneburg family and their wishes; for the Elector, notwithstanding his avoidance of politics, was susceptible on the subject of his army, and averse to being deprived of the thews and sinews of war.

If dismay had been the only feeling prevalent in the ultra-Tory camp, it would have been well for Bolingbroke. But resentment, unfortunately, reared its head in the House of Commons, and a compact Cave of Adullam—the name by which, thanks to Mr. Bright's wit, we moderns know such political sections—was formed, containing amongst others, Lockhart of Carnwarth, a Scotch Jacobite of position and influence in Lanarkshire, but who knew little of England, and the Sir John Pakington of that day.

These malcontents proceeded to join the Whigs in voting against the supplies, and adopted tactics of a nature which, in later days, have unfortunately become familiar to modern Englishmen.* Bolingbroke resolved to see Lockhart, and, if possible,

* 'Lockhart Papers,' vol. i. p. 476. Two other Tories, viz. Sir W. Wyndham and Mr. Secretary Bromley, were not above speaking against time when it suited their purpose.—Ibid., p. 458.

persuade him to allow public business to proceed, using as an argument that continued opposition of this description could only result in the collapse of Lord Oxford's Administration. Bolingbroke expressed himself as ill-satisfied with the personal conduct of the First Minister, yet maintained that the confusion certain to ensue on his downfall was likely to effect no good and to thwart the Queen, who could and would settle matters in such a way "that she would be at liberty to do what she pleased, and being once done, the Parliament might again be re-assembled in a little time to ratify and approve her proceedings."

Bolingbroke proceeded to argue that many would come over to us when they saw *the thing* done, and the *game* secured.

What the *thing* and the *game* might be, this politic Minister does not seem to have whispered even to his staunch supporter;* for Lockhart adds: "'Tis true indeed that his Lordship did not particularly name the King's Restoration," and only confined himself to hints and innuendoes.

It will occur to our readers that if any such wild design was afoot in 1714 as that of calling on the Legislature to change the Succession and disinherit the Protestant branch, who had been deliberately chosen by Parliament as heads of the Royal House of England, there could have been small motive for concealment when such a partisan as Lockhart was

* 'Lockhart Papers,' vol. i. p. 477.

in question—a man, be it remembered, in the closest confidence with St. Germain, and to whom for years to come James Edward used to write letters.

But despite his success with Lockhart's recalcitrant friends, Lord Bolingbroke knew that no temporary device could prevent a serious split in the Tory ranks, and it came sooner than was expected. The knowledge of quarrels in the Cabinet, and a distrust evinced by men such as Shrewsbury, Nottingham, and Somerset, had convinced the rank and file that something was wrong in the camp. Moderate men of the party trusted neither Oxford nor Bolingbroke, and knowing the irreparable breach between the Tory leaders, were daily looking for that dismemberment of the Cabinet which became more probable day by day, and indeed the mutual recriminations of the two statesmen contained statements assuming implication in treasonable designs against the Succession which were enough to destroy confidence in the hearts of strong men, and raise up fears in the hearts of weak ones.

Hence occurred a whole crop of secessions, especially in the House of Lords, where the immediate safety of the Brunswick Settlement was confirmed by a majority of twelve only. Amongst the first to secede was the Earl of Anglesea, and the abovementioned Sir William Dawes, esteemed the most eloquent Churchman in England.*

* For a notice of the Archbishop, see J. H. Overton's 'Life in the English Church,' 1660–1714, p. 254.

Shortly after the whole bench of Bishops were found in opposition, together with the Earls of Abingdon and Jersey, the latter being a Jacobite and Catholic peer whose wife had been under the Abbé Gaultier's spiritual direction when he announced the English desire for peace to M. de Torcy.

The Lords Ashburnham and Carteret, together with Sir Thomas Hanmer, followed suit soon after; and despite the fact that Lord Oxford's fall was apparent to those familiar with the Court intrigues of Mrs. Masham, yet there was a distinct disinclination to entrust Bolingbroke with the leadership. He was neither reckoned to be a man of sufficient character, nor did he possess the favour of the City, where capitalists viewed with disfavour a peace that had limited their field of profitable investment by prohibiting additions to the national debt; and yet it had been as the chosen champions of such unscientific commercial ideas that Godolphin and Marlborough floated down the tide of popularity and glory, which enabled them to cripple Louis the Fourteenth.

There is nothing more unstable than the cohesion of a parliamentary majority, however apparently numerous or secure; for excuses will speedily be found to cabal, abstain, or in the last resort go into active opposition whenever they see that a Minister's errors are recognised by the same public opinion that endowed him with power. The dispersion of such authority is generally gradual at first, beginning, may be, with the defection of a leading colleague, whom after a brief interval others follow readily when they find their chief's power departing and see an unrelenting enemy scaling the party citadel.

To put off such an evil day as this did the Oxford Administration disgrace its memory, by proposing and carrying the Schism Bill in both Houses. The House of Peers, it should be remembered to their credit, showed more favour to religious liberty than the more popular chamber, where 237 members decided to refuse Dissenters the right of educating their children, except in the principles of the Established Church, while a minority of 208 were not prepared to infringe the principles of growing toleration which had rendered the Revolution of 1688 possible.

In the House of Lords the retrograde measure was only carried by five; but Bolingbroke's purpose was temporarily gained, and the High Church Tories by remaining firm saved the Ministry.* But men were uncomfortably exercised in mind as to what Bolingbroke and those who followed him might do next, and no inconsiderable portion of his thoughtful countrymen, rightly or wrongly, jumped to the conclusion that the step in question might be that of restoring the Pretender. As the majority of his-

* The demise of the Queen, which occurred shortly after, rendered this measure a dead-letter, and the Whigs, of course, never revived a statute justly abhorrent to their principles.—See continuation of Sir J. Mackintosh's 'History,' vol. ix. pp. 319–20.

torians have recorded the several indications which point towards the Tory Government of Lord Oxford favouring the Jacobites, and being prepared, under certain given circumstances, to take measures calculated to sustain their leader's claim to be crowned at Westminster Abbey, so in the interest of justice and equity is it desirable to show what wild Whig schemes were likewise in the air, to take effect when their cause could be supported no longer by constitutional means.

We put aside as doubtful the story, that when Prince Eugene was in London during 1711 to prevent the English from making peace with France unless the Imperial claims were satisfied, Marlborough and Eugene were designing to burn London if they could not persuade the Queen and her Ministers to continue the war. This statement, which appears in Macpherson's 'Original Papers,' Dean Swift has revived in his 'Last Four Years of Queen Anne's Reign,' being likewise re-echoed in various partisan narratives, but it has not been clearly verified, and the whole story bears evidence of unreality, resting on the *ipse dixit* of one Plunket, a Jesuit, and finding no support elsewhere.

It is different in regard to the inflamed condition of the Whig party after Lord Bolingbroke brought in his Schism Bill in 1714. Lockhart, who was certainly a shrewd observer when his master's cause was in question, heard enough in and around St. Stephen's to convince him that the Jacobite hopes, even if the Ministry favoured them—which he doubted—were destined to rude dispersal. Money was collected in considerable quantities for the purpose of purchasing arms and ammunition, and stranger than all,

> "They caused make severall thousand figures of a small fusie about two inches long in brass, and some few in silver and gold, which were to be dispersed amongst the chiefs and more zealous of the partie as a signal in the day of tryall." *

Lockhart got possession of three of these fusees, and sent one to Mary of Modena by Lord Mar. Another he tied by a small ribbon in the breast of his coat, and placed himself in the House of Commons near a Whig kinsman and friend, Sir Robert Pollock, who gazed on the bauble with amazement, and when the wily Lockhart pretended to hide it, said, "either our secrets are discovered, or you're a convert." It is possible that the Whig leaders did contemplate the Electoral Prince appearing in London with an armed escort variously appraised as to strength, while we shall not stop to record here all that Lockhart's exaggerated fears led him to credit concerning this raising of armies at home and abroad to intimidate Queen Anne at St. James's,† but the latter rumours are neither more nor less credible than other unauthenticated statements which charge direct hostility to the House of Brunswick against the Tory

* 'Lockhart Papers,' vol. i. p. 463.

† According to Plunket's apocryphal account, re-echoed in Swift's 'Last Four Years of Queen Anne,' 50,000 men under Marlborough and Eugene were to force Queen Anne to carry on the Whig war policy.

Ministry of 1710–14. How far they apparently went in the direction of St. Germain and where they stopped, is, however, traced carefully in these pages. One thing is perfectly certain, the Whigs themselves suffered from genuine apprehension; General Stanhope, for instance, was in despair, and told Lockhart in Westminster Hall, "Well, you'll get your Pretender;" * while not only was the veteran Somers recalled to the Whig conclaves, but the general public conception of the situation justified their alarms.

It is pretty well known that the Queen had decided to allow the parliamentary law of Succession to remain undisturbed, directly she learnt that her brother was immovable in the matter of religion; but a conversation she held with her half-sister's husband, Sheffield, Duke of Buckingham, tells the story in all its fulness.

The Duke had offered his hand to the Princess Anne before her marriage with the Prince of Denmark, but ultimately united himself with Catherine Darnley, natural daughter of James the Second by Catherine Sedley. This relationship entitled Buckingham to an intimacy with the Sovereign, and being a friend to James Edward's succession, despite several asseverations to Hanover, the Duke urged her brother's cause on Queen Anne during a conversation held in the year 1712, and received the following reply:—

* 'Lockhart Papers,' vol. i. p. 479.

"You see he doth not make the least step to oblige me. I have no reason to think he values me or my estate, and therefore I am determined to give it to Hanover." *

The Duke of Buckingham having protested that no such obligation existed, and stated his belief that the son of James the Second was ready to give securities, his Royal sister-in-law answered as follows:—

"What wouldst thou have me do. As the law stands a Papist cannot inherit, and therefore should I alter my will, it would be to no purpose, the law will give it all to Hanover, and therefore I had better do that with a good grace which I cannot help."

The original desire of Queen Anne to restore her brother is one of those facts in history which no student can doubt; but her steady resolve to sustain the Church of England as a Protestant establishment outlived the earlier family sentiment, and is stamped indelibly on the records of her later life. But the statement of Queen Anne concerning the Succession, which has far more weight than any other, was voluntarily made to Sir William Dawes, the Archbishop of York, after that popular and eloquent prelate had seceded from the Tories in April, 1714, on the ground that he believed the Brunswick family were in danger of losing their rights as heads of the Protestant branch. According to the statement of Mr. John Chamberlayne, who had been the late Prince George of Denmark's Master of the House-

* Macpherson's 'Original Papers,' Stuart collection, vol. ii. p. 328.

hold, Her Majesty desired to see the Archbishop, who straightway set forth the people's "fears and jealousies" concerning the Pretender, receiving for reply the most solemn assurances binding the Queen to preserve the Protestant Succession as by Parliament established, "cultivating the same both by herself and her Ministers." *

* We give the letter in full as it is one of the most important amongst the Hanover Papers, and has not hitherto been published :—

"Westminster, April 27, 1714.

"Your Royal Highness having lately given me a new mark of your Favor by ordering your secretary to tell me that you have prevailed on his Electoral Highness to suffer me most humbly to lay at his Feet the next Edition of my State of Great Britain, I find myself obliged to approach your Illustrious person with fresh Acknowledgments of the same which I now do with the utmost Deference and Respect, and with exceeding great Pleasure, tho' I am almost ashamed to be so often Troublesome to so Great a Princess. *And perhaps Madam I should not have ventured to trouble your Highness so soon upon this occasion only if the Archbishop of York (than whom there is no Man in England more Devoted to your interest) had not acquainted me in a private conversation this day, and allow'd me at the same time to inform your Highness that her Majesty sent for him very lately, and permitted him with great Liberty, and with that Candor and Sincerity that is natural to his Grace, to lay before her his thoughts of the People's Fears and Jealousys concerning the Pretender, and of the dangers to the Succession so much apprended* (sic) *by all good Protestants. And after that her Majesty had heard him with Great Patience and Attention, she was pleased to give him the most solemn Assurances of her sincere and unalterable Affection to your Highness and your most illustrious Family and Resolutions of cultivating the same both by herself and her Ministers.*

"But Madam what I now take the Liberty to inform your R.H., tho it be as full an account as I dare charge an imperfect and bad Memory with, yet is far short of what his Grace will inform you himself whenever you please to command that of him, and why should not your R.H. condescend to Ask it of him. In truth Madam your Highness will always be sure by his means of the Hearts of almost all our Clergy, which Argument is most Humbly submitted by

"Madam of your Royal Highness

"The most Faithful, Devoted and obliged servant,

"JOHN CHAMBERLAYNE."

Various were the efforts made to induce James Edward to rescind the resolve which precluded any dissembling as regards religion. Netterville, a Jesuit of position, thought that the Pope might with advantage give the assumedly rightful English King a dispensation for turning Protestant. In fact

"he would oblige the King to declare himself a Protestant, being the safest way to secure the crown, and establish the Roman Catholic religion in England, and when he compleats the work appear with safety in his true shape and not be beholden to anybody." *

Such were the devices abroad to justify religious pretence at Bar-le-Duc, while the English Ministry were straining every nerve to sustain their power.

The aforesaid Netterville proposed to Harley, in 1713, that he should abolish triennial Parliaments, and so anticipate Walpole †—a suggestion placed aside by the unfathomable Lord Treasurer averring that such a measure threatened to be too violent, and that there was reason to believe the next Parliament would equal its predecessor in Tory virtues.

But, hand in hand with all this plotting and counter-plotting, a feeling of distrust permeated the nation, and finds expression in the papers preserved at the Record Office which have reference to this peculiar and momentous period—the last two years of Queen Anne's reign.

* Macpherson's 'Original Papers,' vol. ii. p. 399.

† Ibid., p. 393.

Parties seem to have been terribly embittered ; unbeneficed clergymen being turned out of their cures because they held political opinions contrary to those of their patrons, clerical or lay ; while reports of treasonable sayings regarding the Pretender were abroad, such accusations being apparently straightway submitted to the law-officers of the Crown. On the other hand, we learn that a man speaking improperly regarding the execution of Charles the First was adjudged by the Attorney-General to have committed misdemeanour, not high treason ; while no quarter was shown to the Whig pamphleteer, Daniel De Foe, who, being the victim of a Crown prosecution, soon deserted politics to the manifest enrichment of a contemporary literature already sufficiently famous.*

Again, one Patrick Phelan escapes permanent imprisonment for having tarried at St. Germain—an exercise of mercy somewhat strained in its nature, considering that nothing beyond mere sojourn was alleged against him, although a Whig official of that date would probably have viewed with suspicion, rather than as an earnest of respectability, the fact that the detained Irishman had formerly served the French Marshal Tallard.†

In March 1713 one Samuel Webber arrived from France, and informed the Ministry that he was cognisant of a French plot to murder Queen

* 'State Papers.' Anne. Domestic Series, bundle 29.

† Ibid.

Anne; but owing to certain doubts as to Webber's character which kind friends of his disseminated—apparently not without a substratum of truth—this unfortunate individual was kept in durance vile pending inquiries made in Tipperary, where he was a proprietor of land. Although Webber did not come well out of the inquiry in question, and his story concerning the plot was adjudged unreliable, yet the memoranda in the Record Office relating thereto are worth repeating.

He writes to Lord Dartmouth, one of the Secretaries of State, speaking of the dangers to which his family are exposed in Ireland owing to his having disclosed a Jacobite plot against Queen Anne, "it being," he says, "too common in Ireland to fire the houses or hough the chattle (*sic*) in the feild of such they envie."

Mr. Webber expresses a wish, which will doubtless be echoed by any modern Irish landlords circumstanced as he then was, viz. to settle in the West of England. Mr. Webber's release seems to have been coincident with the discrediting of his plot against the Queen's life, but we are not told what was his future in the wilds of Tipperary.

However, the advices from Ireland continue to be extremely interesting. An anonymous correspondent writes that unless some colonels and field officers were changed, the troops quartered there were not all to be depended on, one Fort-Major Wyndham being charged with toasting the Pretender at an entertainment given in Kinsale by General Nicholson, the designer of the futile expedition to Canada. As a remedy against the discontent and distrust prevailing in the Emerald Isle, the often-mooted idea of a regiment of Irish Guards being formed was recommended, while expression is given to a fear, generally entertained amongst the Whigs, lest Parliament should repeal the Triennial Act.*

But these were not the only indications of the activity of those who desired to create a Jacobite panic, and compel the Ministry to put in force the laws against the Roman Catholics. Letters were simultaneously received by the Mayors of York, Exeter, Oxford, and Hereford, "exhorting them to use their utmost endeavour to persuade their citizens to declare for King James the Third as their rightful and lawful king." The document averred that,

> "the Queen had given leave for the French ambassador to rise (*sic*) a regiment of 1000 men here in England for the King's guards to attend him on his landing and 700 is already listed and quartered about Southwark."

It ended by declaring that,

> "Sir Patrick Curtis, once the King's envoy at Madrid, is now his envoy here at the court of England. Therefore the Queen and her Ministry agreeing you are to choose fit men to carry the work through."

* 'State Papers.' Anne. Domestic Series, bundle 29. May 1713. The Whigs in Ireland threatened that the Duke of Hanover and the Duke of Marlborough would soon come and save the kingdom from the "dangers it's running into whether the Queen or Parliament will or no."

Finally, just after Parliament had been dissolved in August 1713, and the Tories returned triumphantly, the elections being carried in four places out of five by the Ministry, there is an account given by one De Saulac, who, taken into custody for toasting James the Third, and presumably to secure his liberty, gave information of another plot, which in this case seems to have had a slight foundation. According to De Saulac, 20,000 men were prepared to rise in Scotland, while a simultaneous movement took place round London. If this rebellion succeeded, De Saulac was to be Gentleman of the Horse. A Jesuit, by name Campbell, was concerned, and a ship, with men and ammunition, was expected at Poole, in Dorsetshire, where the Record Office Papers tell us there had been a seizure of Popish documents four months before. When prevented from landing at Poole, the strange craft put out to sea, and is said ultimately to have reached Kirkaldy, in Fifeshire, where her crew went ashore.* No mention of any such expedition finds place in the various Jacobite memoirs, but we give De Saulac's story as a sample of the kind of rumour that helped to create an impression—in the minds of a minority, which accorded with their hopes and wishes—to wit, that Oxford and Bolingbroke were bent on restoring James Edward Stuart. And of course their power being strengthened by the recent general election for three years, more than ever impressed onlookers

* 'State Papers.' Anne. Domestic Series, bundle 31. Oct. 1713.

with the idea that this great change was to be brought about.

We have elsewhere given an opinion that Ministers collectively desired to keep the Tory party in office rather than alter the Succession, and that, to do Lord Oxford justice, his original pourparlers with the Jacobite agents meant no more than that he could ill afford to lose some forty votes in the House of Commons, while even if the falling Minister—for his differences with Mrs. Masham, Queen Anne's favourite, and his desperate quarrel with Bolingbroke, were undermining the authority which, as Lord Treasurer, he still held—did once conceive the possibility of a Restoration, it was not that of a Roman Catholic sovereign to tenant Windsor, and fill once more with ecclesiastical satellites the galleries of Whitehall and St. James's.

There seems to be no doubt that, after Oxford's fall, Bolingbroke had resolved to do the best in his power to carry out the Parliamentary decision, and bring George the First to St. James's, while Mr. Drummond, his particular friend, was instructed to repair to Holland, and smooth the way for such a programme if the Queen died.

Arthur Moore was presumably to have been Chancellor of the Exchequer; Sir William Wyndham, leader of the House of Commons; and Marlborough —if he would accept the position under Bolingbroke —General-in-Chief of the Forces; while Ormond was to be relegated to the Lord-Lieutenancy of

Ireland, or be left out altogether if he refused the position.

Ormond was an irreconcilable enemy to Marlborough, and it is certain that he, too, for a time believed it was wise to accept the inevitable, and pay court to the rising sun, inasmuch as in the Hanover Papers there are two letters, dated respectively June 18, and September 5, 1714, in which devotion to the House of Brunswick is expressed by Ormond, the prince of Jacobite intriguers, who, to do him justice, risked everything for the Stuarts, and, as we shall show, had their interests at heart when the crucial moment arrived.

The authority upon which this opinion regarding Bolingbroke's later design is founded is the evidence of Thomas Carte's 'Contemporary Note-book,' now in the Bodleian Library at Oxford, extracts from which Macpherson has placed amongst his 'Original Papers.'*

There was no quarrel between Marlborough and Bolingbroke which was not capable of adjustment,†

* Vol. ii. pp. 527–534. There is a note in the Onslow copy of Burnet's 'History,' written in Lord Hardwick's hand, to the following effect:—

"The Speaker (Mr. Onslow) has told me, that he had been informed by the late Lord Orford (Sir R. Walpole) and Arthur Moore, that Lord Bolingbroke had formed a scheme of administration upon the turning out the Earl of Oxford by which he was to have been Lord Treasurer, Sir William Wyndham, one of the Secretaries of State, and Arthur Moore, Chancellor of the Exchequer; and it is now generally believed that the Duke of Marlborough was to have been restored to the Command of the army."

† Macpherson's 'History of England,' vol. ii. p. 651; also Despatch of Mr. St. John to Duke of Marlborough, July 31, 1711, quoted in Alison's 'Marlborough,' vol. ii. p. 195.

and although it does not seem possible to prove absolute collusion between these two men of genius, there is every reason to believe they would have acted cordially together had their interests become identical.

As regards Thomas Carte's 'Note-book,' if Professor Gardiner sees his way to use that antiquarian's *researches* for historical purposes, as he has done in his last work, there can exist no bar to judicious use being made of the said contemporary chronicles, which point to conclusions of a character that a Jacobite and a Jesuit could scarcely have desired. In fact, Carte's wish was not father to the thought in question. But until the circumstances connected with Lord Clarendon's mission to Hanover have been duly related, it is not advisable to attempt a solution of this many-sided problem.

CHAPTER X.

LORD CLARENDON'S MISSION TO HANOVER.

APRIL TO SEPTEMBER, 1714.

THE political condition of Europe just before Queen Anne's death ought, in justice to George the First, to be noticed in any account of the manner in which his family attained the throne.

Among those of the Hanover Papers which deal with the later years of Queen Anne's reign, there are several allusions to the Elector's refusal to find money for diplomatic purposes; and historians of the highest capacity have therefore allowed the charge of meanness to go by default, while they explain his lack of power to excite enthusiasm amongst parties in England by the existence of this blot on his character.

Now, before registering any such hasty judgment in his own mind, let the reader take the Elector of Hanover's European position into consideration. What chance was there of his receiving quarter from his enemies on the Continent, if, jealous of the position of the Brunswick-Luneburg family in

Northern Europe, they found George Lewis with an impoverished treasury, and confronted by an England which had restored the Pretender?

France certainly would have hailed such a situation with delight, while both Spain and Portugal were under the influence of Louis the Fourteenth; Philip the Fifth, monarch of the former country, "nourishing a violent antipathy to the Elector himself."* Nor could much be expected from Charles the Sixth, head of the House of Austria, who at the Peace of Rastadt, signed on March 6, 1714, between France and the Empire, declined to guarantee the Succession in England to the Brunswick family, and was by no means unwilling to marry a daughter to the Chevalier de St. George.† Russia, it is true, owing to a war with Sweden and Turkey, had not yet taken up the hostile attitude which the Czar Peter shortly displayed towards Hanoverian interests generally;‡ while the United Provinces, wearied out by exertions beyond their strength, and deeply in debt, gave a sympathy to the Brunswick cause, which circumstances did not allow them to render effective. Charles the Twelfth, irritated at the Elector's claim to Bremen and Verden, was avowedly hostile to the Brunswick Succession; while Augustus the Second of Poland grovelled at the feet of Peter the Great,

* Coxe's 'Walpole,' vol. i. p. 52.

† Macpherson's 'Original Papers,' vol. ii. p. 523. The Imperial envoy at Vienna told the Duke of Lorraine that the Emperor "seemed to relish the proposal."

‡ Coxe's 'Walpole,' vol. i. pp. 94, 181.

who had made him king. Denmark, although under Frederick the Fourth, a passive friend to the Protestant cause, yet looked rather to accept assistance from George than to render it to him when need arose. Nor is it possible to deny that a dangerous ally might have been obtained by any enemy of Hanover in the person of that inconstant sovereign, Victor Amadeus, Duke of Savoy, who, although the Treaty of Utrecht had given him Sicily, part of Milan, and a promise of the Spanish Crown when Philip the Fifth's male line failed, yet felt aggrieved that his wife, Anna Maria, great granddaughter of Charles the First of England, had been passed over in favour of the Elector of Hanover.* No long time after, this discontented prince reverted to his old connection with France. Prussia, under Frederick William the First, who had not yet matured the military force which rendered the nation so strong in the ensuing reign of Frederick the Great, was a *bonâ fide* friend to the Electoral cause. But his whole force, though valuable doubtless on the defensive when in alliance with the gallant Hanoverians, could not be expected to enable the Elector to resist successfully a possible coalition such as the position of James Edward on the British throne must have induced him to organise. Finally, we may remember that although the temporal power of Clement XI. was at a low ebb, yet the tendency of his spiritual authority must necessarily have

* Coxe's 'Walpole,' vol. i. p. 54.

been directed towards keeping a Catholic Stuart at Windsor.

Therefore we consider that the Elector acted only with proper circumspection when he kept money in his purse, and refused to impoverish the land of his birth, when adherents such as Schutz and Bothmar thought his hopes so uncertain. On the other hand, he gave an impression to onlookers that he was somewhat indifferent about mounting the British throne, which, although his mother, then in her eighty-fourth year, might rest thereon for a while, was looked on as destined to be soon tenanted by George Lewis himself.

He would neither grant pensions, nor influence the elections with money; he rejected the violent proposals made, strange to say, by the Whigs at this time, to bring foreign troops into the English kingdom, and finally only gave way regarding the writ summoning his son, the Electoral Prince, to England, when satisfied, as we have shown, that the alternative would probably be a Catholic Restoration in England followed by a continental invasion of Brunswick-Luneburg and its territories,* planned in collusion with the triumphant Stuarts.

Therefore George Lewis and his mother could not remain unmoved when it was announced that the Pretender was meditating an incursion into England, where not only his supporters, but even the German agents, thought he would be received with acclaim.

* Macpherson's 'Original Papers,' vol. ii. p. 520.

Above all, they persuaded themselves that at last James the Second's son had cast aside present scruples as to changing his religion. Whether he were acting *bonâ fide* in the matter, or, in accordance with the advice given by the Jesuit Netterville, quietly dissembling, mattered not to the frenzied foreigners who stood responsible for the management of the Hanoverian diplomacy.

The truth, however, was that, notwithstanding the conspicuous favour shown personally to the famous Protestant non-juror Charles Leslie, the Pretender never allowed this potent ally to do more than hold a service in a back room at Bar-le-Duc, and soon repented of having yielded even to that extent.*

We have seen how electrical was the political atmosphere in England, and the state of affairs became more and more critical,† as the Queen grew feebler in health. The mutual recriminations of Oxford and Bolingbroke, wherein, as has been

* Harrop's 'Bolingbroke,' p. 196, quoting Lathbury's 'History of the Non-Jurors.'

† As a specimen of the many false alarms abroad we may mention one that reached the Mayor of Dover in July 1714, to the effect that men were being deported from Ireland and Scotland to join the Pretender at Havre, where 40,000 men were to embark. When this matter came to be looked into by Sir E. Northey, the Attorney-General, it was discovered that four men enlisted for the Pretender were interviewed at Havre, and that some suspicious craft had been seen in the Downs flying French colours, while one barque had approached Eastbourne and carried on some smuggling transactions with the inhabitants. (See Domestic Papers, Anne, 1714, Record Office, bundle 30.) A conspiracy this on an even more minute scale than even Lord Wharton's, when the two Kellys enlisting men for James Edward led to that unfortunate Prince being proclaimed by Parliament, and a price set on his head if he visited British soil.

said, neither statesman refrained from accusing the other of a design to change the Succession and bring in James Edward without securities, had been reported to Bernsdorff and Robethon at Herrenhausen.

In consequence of the impression made upon the Hanoverian diplomatists, the letters of Robethon at Herrenhausen, Kreyenberg in London, and Bothmar at the Hague, became quite dramatic, and it is clear that they distrusted the English Cabinet thoroughly. Bolingbroke's direct appeal for confidence at Herrenhausen had been made as early as October 1710, and was so far appreciated that the Elector returned a polite answer referring to Bolingbroke's influence with the Queen, and speaking of the esteem and regard with which he was looked on at the Electoral Court, but declining nevertheless to correspond except through Baron Bothmar. As it was apparently impossible to get on to a better footing than the one described, Lord Oxford's Administration betook themselves to the device of a diplomatic mission,* Thomas Harley, brother of the Premier, being chosen for the post of envoy. When at Hanover, in May 1714, Mr. Harley was startled by receiving a joint memorial from the Elector and his mother the Electress,

* Previous experience had not been such as to give much encouragement to this method of procedure. In 1711 Lord Rivers was despatched to Hanover with an assurance to the Elector that his succession to the crown should be secured in the treaty; in reply to which the Electoral Court represented the pernicious consequences of Philip's remaining in possession of Spain and the West Indies. Bothmar published this remonstrance, and so gave deep offence at Queen Anne's Court.

"desiring the Pretender's removal into Italy from Lorraine. A pension for the Princess Sophia. Leave to send a Prince of the Electoral family to Britain, and titles as Princes of the Blood to those protestant Princes who were without such honours." *

This was the first gust which betokened a coming storm, and indicated a resolve on the part of Robethon's correspondents to bring matters concerning the residence of the Electoral Prince in England to an issue.

But Thomas Harley played a card which created a counter-excitement in the enemies' camp, when he produced original letters of Marlborough's to the Pretender, with which the crafty Prime Minister had armed his brother before allowing him to depart on his mission.†

Well might Bothmar with amazement compare these epistles with effusive passages of anger and contempt against the Jacobites which Marlborough had again and again penned to the Elector's Ministers.

Meantime the situation in England had developed, and necessitated urgent measures on the part of Government. At a meeting held at Lord Halifax's, the Whig junto, or such part of it as could be collected, had resolved to persuade Schutz, the Hanoverian Minister in London, to demand a writ for the

* 'Hanover Papers,' Strafford, 1714.

† This is on the whole one of the most important disclosures in the Hanover Papers. It is described in Macpherson's 'Original Papers,' vol ii. p. 638.

Electoral Prince, so that he might straightway reside in England.

Schutz had asked for this writ on the 12th of April, 1714, and from that moment the Queen resolved that there should be no mistake as to her own views of the question at issue. Lord Clarendon, the Minister chosen to proceed upon this delicate mission, had, as Lord Cornbury, been Governor of Pennsylvania, and during his sojourn there had instituted postal arrangements between England and that colony. Bothmar, believing that Lord Bolingbroke had chosen Lord Clarendon,* sneered at the new envoy, speaking of him with strange inaccuracy as a Governor appointed to the Indies, where, to represent his Queen, he was said to have dressed himself up as a woman: an unsupported story which has been re-echoed by several writers on the *ipse dixit* of this interested partisan.

There were, however, as the next few pages will show, good reasons why the Ministry selected Lord Clarendon to take up the threads, and communicate to the authorities at Herrenhausen Queen Anne's unflinching resolve not to acquiesce in a successor's residence in England during her own lifetime.

But ten days before this mission was announced by letters to the Court of Hanover, the aged Electress passed away suddenly while walking in the

* "Lord Oxford told me the day before yesterday, as he spoke to me of Lord Clarendon's departure, that he knew very well his Lordship would not speak well of him at Hanover, a certain sign that it is Bolingbroke who sent him."—Kreyenberg to Robethon, 'Hanover Papers,' July, 1714.

gardens of Herrenhausen.* She had strongly championed the project of sending the Electoral Prince to England, and in her last few weeks took more active measures on behalf of her family prospects than any she had participated in during her whole previous career. A cultured, high-minded woman, she would, no doubt, have adapted herself to English customs, and fulfilled a royal position in London as became the descendant of Henry the Lion and the Scotch Stuarts. A due estimate of her character will have been gathered from an earlier portion of this volume; and beyond the fact that her interest in the Brunswick Succession increased as years passed on, there is nothing new to chronicle here of this excellent lady, who died at the ripe age of 84.

Before Lord Clarendon's departure, the offending Hanoverian agent, Schutz, was driven from his post by the English Ministry. He was destined to be the scapegoat selected to suffer the Royal displeasure, and a careful perusal of the Hanover Papers that bear reference to this matter has convinced us that if Queen Anne had lived, and the Court of Herrenhausen proved obdurate, something akin to civil war would have been kindled in England.†

* Some writers have suggested that the tenor of Queen Anne's letters had disturbed the Electress so much, that vexation and agitation combined caused heart complaint to become acute.

† The Ministerial letters which appear in the 'Hanover Papers' are described in the 'English Historical Review,' vol. i. p. 772. The ensuing account of the mission of Lord Clarendon was written by the author when fresh from study of the 'Hanover Papers,' and is substantially narrated in the text.

In her letter to the Electress, the Queen spoke thus of the project to which she desired to take the strongest exception possible: "plus dangereux a la tranquillite de mes etats, au Droit de la succession dans votre ligne." Mr. Secretary Bromley's letter, which accompanied that of Queen Anne, contained the following passage:—

"Your Lordship will endeavour to satisfy the Elector the Queen has no intention, but to secure the Succession to her Crowns as by law established in the house of Hanover and is ready to do everything that may contribute to that end consistent with the safe and quiet possession of them during her own time. Her Majesty having been very sincere in the public declarations she has made, and in the assurances she has frequently given in favour of this succession; she expects from the Elector he will speak freely on this subject, and particularly if he thinks he has reason to suspect designs are carrying on to disappoint it, that he will declare what foundation he has for such suspicion.

"And your Lordship will assure him he may depend that no person shall be continued in her Majesty's service he has reasonable ground to imagine has other views, and if that can be made appear her Majesty will not fail to make examples of such persons.

"Upon your Lordship's arrival at Hanover you will learn what resolution that Court has taken about the Electoral Prince [the Duke of Cambridge] coming hither, the demanding the writ for his sitting in Parliament having given an expectation it was soon intended. Your Lordship will find such resolution is either taken or suspended, or a resolution taken that he will not come over without her Majesty's consent and invitation.

"If the resolution for his coming is taken or suspended your Lordship will represent to the Elector, the great uneasiness his coming hither at this time will give the Queen, how unreasonable it is, and that it may endanger the succession itself."

Lord Clarendon reached the Hague, after experiencing some delay, on July 17, and was in Hanover on the 31st. Shortly after his arrival he received a letter, dated July 27, announcing that the Lord Treasurer had been dismissed, but that the incident should make no alteration with respect to public affairs. For the moment no Lord Treasurer was to be appointed, but the office placed in commission.

A delay of several days ensued after sending in his credentials to the Elector, and Lord Clarendon remained at Hanover until an interview could be arranged. The King of Prussia was in conclave with his brother-in-law, George Lewis, so it was not until August 3 that Lord Clarendon even saw Baron Bernsdorff, who, explaining the cause of delay, promised that coaches should be in readiness to carry him to Herrenhausen directly the King of Prussia had left.

This occurred on August 7, when George Lewis not only received Lord Clarendon with cordiality, but soon put it beyond doubt that he intended to conform to Her Majesty's desire in the matter of the writ. He told Lord Clarendon that the idea of the Electoral Prince's sojourn in England had commended itself to the late Electress, but that in asking for the writ, Schutz had acted without her cognizance and on his own responsibility.

In fact, he threw his agent over altogether, a solution that must have proved distasteful to the Whig party, had not events straightway declared for the cause they championed. The Elector spoke thus plainly concerning his own innocence: "J'espere que le Reine n'a pas cru que cela y'est fait par mon ordre. Je vous assure cela a este fait a mon insceu."

Had Queen Anne lived, in what a false position would the Whig party in England have been placed by this surrender, when Bernsdorff, Bothmar, and Robethon, together with all the Hanoverian agents then in power, were acting in collusion!

Lord Clarendon told Bernsdorff, without receiving a word in reply, that "it was the more necessary for the Elector to enter into an entire confidence with the Queen as the surest means to secure his interest against the Pretender."

Such was the situation when, after a premonitory warning sent from St. James's, the news of the Queen's death reached Hanover on August 17th. Lord Clarendon, seeking a fresh audience of the Elector, communicated to him the fact; to which George the First replied, that the account tallied with that which Robethon had received.

Lord Clarendon then asked for instructions, and was desired to stay in Hanover until the King set out for his English dominions.

The Hanover Papers, from which we have evolved this account, tell us that no hesitation ensued in any quarter except as regards the King's departure, which, although it was delayed seven weeks, was immediately provided for by the British Minister at the Hague, who while informing the new Sovereign of his devotion, told him also that the *Peregrine*,* the best Royal yacht, was awaiting him on the coast of Holland.

We have dwelt somewhat in detail on this mission of Lord Clarendon's, because its import seems to have been overlooked amidst the frequent recitals of more stirring scenes nearer home† In spite of the delay, which was doubtless designed to make the ground sure in London, and to benefit by the prescient forethought of Lord Somers, when he appointed a Regency during the King's enforced absence on the Continent, there was not a ripple on the flowing stream which bore the Brunswick family to the honour they so well deserved. But the smooth surface of the waters might at any moment have been transformed into a whirlpool, for it is well known that had Atterbury been a soldier or a statesman instead of a Bishop, he would have put his opinions to the test of civil war, while not even did his sacred office prevent him from avowing his desire to proclaim the Pretender at Charing Cross in full canonicals.‡

* The *Peregrine* was built by the Marquess of Carmarthen for William the Third, and was accounted one of the finest craft in the service. The Marquess was promised £1000 a year as a compensation for his design, together with time and money expended, but never received it, the Government apparently making the exorbitant price charged an excuse for not paying at all. Although a legal re-assignment of the *Peregrine* was made to the Marquess of Carmarthen, the Admiralty refused to part with the vessel, and, as we have stated, it brought George the First to England.—'Record Office Papers,' Domestic Series. Anne, bundle 30.

† The poet Gay acted as Lord Clarendon's secretary during this mission.

‡ This fact has stood the test of Mr. W. H. Lecky's research. Lecky's 'History of England in the Eighteenth Century,' vol. i. p. 166.

Moreover there were laymen of quality who would gladly have followed him. Mr. Carte, in his memorandum book, which is at the Bodleian Library, is said to have received the following anecdote from the Duke of Ormond :—

"The night before the Queen died, when the Council broke up the Duke of Buckingham came to the Duke of Ormond, clapped his hand on his shoulder and said, My Lord, you have twenty-four hours' time to do our business in and make yourself master of the kingdom."

But the twenty-four hours passed by without any such action taking place,* so that Somers' organisation being perfected, peace was preserved, and the Brunswick family came to the British throne without a drop of blood being spilt, and if it had been possible for them to have adopted a national, instead of a party policy, the sad story of 1715 perhaps need never have been told.†

* It is worth while observing that there is no historical foundation for the idea that James Edward was in England at this juncture, of which Thackeray has made such effective use in the charming romance of 'Esmond.'

† According to Carte, the Queen relented as to her brother before she died, sending for the Bishop of London, and making a sort of confession to him. The Bishop is said to have replied aloud before the Duchess of Ormond and others: "I'll declare your mind; but it will cost me my head." If this be true, the Prelate in question had not the resolution to carry out the Queen's behest.—Macpherson's 'Original Papers,' vol. ii. p. 528.

CHAPTER XI.

GEORGE THE FIRST AT ST. JAMES'S.

THE turbulent political scenes which surrounded Queen Anne's last hours were enacted amidst the tremors of a people who believed that they were face to face with the perils incident on a disputed Succession.

Oxford, who had been dismissed ungraciously, soon saw his rival Bolingbroke left far astern in the race for power. At that signally important Council summoned to take the dying Queen's last instructions and to select a Minister in the late Lord Treasurer's place, the Dukes of Somerset and Argyll arrived on the scene * and proposed the Duke of Shrewsbury as holder of the White Staff. Bolingbroke not immediately aspiring to a place his social character precluded him from grasping, yet desired to fill the various offices of State with followers of his own,

* Lord Bolingbroke had made a resolute attempt to conciliate the Whigs the night after Lord Oxford's fall, entertaining Generals Stanhope, Cadogan and Palmes, Sir William Wyndham, Mr. Craggs, and others.—Rapin, vol. xviii. p. 223.

Taken with his expressed desire to unite the leading Tories of all complexions under his banner, there can remain little doubt that a coalition which should keep him in power was the primary object, not the Pretender.

and when the Queen with her dying breath ratified the selection of these two Dukes, all hopes of realising his designs must have vanished even from the mind of England's most eloquent and most energetic statesman; * and he had received this rebuff at the hands of the veteran Shrewsbury, one of those who assisted in bringing about the Revolution of 1688, and yet from time to time corresponded with the son of James the Second.

That Shrewsbury would have registered no antecedent objection to a Stuart restoration is evident from the fact that, as Lord Bolingbroke phrased it, he was *dipped* in Jacobite politics within a few months after the time when he stood in the breach to baulk those far-reaching ambitions, the real nature and full extent of which no man has yet been able to gauge.

Shrewsbury had been for some time out of accord with his political associates, who had looked coldly upon an alliance contracted during a residence in Rome between the Duke and a beautiful Italian girl of humble origin; and his constitutional scruples to Bolingbroke's supremacy were probably seconded by private objections to unhindered Tory pre-eminence. Pointing to Lord Oxford, Bolingbroke had said

* A careful perusal of many accounts of these events and of such MSS. as bear on the subject inclines us on the whole to prefer that by Mr. Robert Harrop in his 'Bolingbroke, a Political Study and Criticism,' pp. 211, 212. He recognises what few other writers do (strange to say, not even Lord Stanhope, notwithstanding his otherwise clear conception of the situation), viz. that the Council and not Bolingbroke were paramount after Oxford's fall.

to Dr. Arbuthnot, the Queen's physician, in July 1714,

"How I stand with that man I know,"

Then pointing to Shrewsbury he added,

"but as to the other I cannot tell."*

Concerning the two nobles whose sudden appearance at the last Council of Queen Anne's reign turned the scale against Bolingbroke, one cannot remain silent.

Charles Seymour, Duke of Somerset, sixth in descent from the great Protector of Edward the Sixth's reign, occupied in the House of Lords much the same position as Harley had formerly filled in the House of Commons. He was the recognised leader of the loyal Tory party which remained faithful to the Protestant Succession, and upon his name no taint of Jacobitism had ever fallen.

Scorning to retain office under James the Second at the expense of his principles, this haughty noble was one of the authors of the great constitutional settlement of 1688, and after William the Third's death was chosen by Queen Anne as her personal friend, although courtier in the ordinary sense of the word it was impossible for him to become.†

So proud was the Duke of Somerset, that he is said to have reprobated the levity of his second wife, a daughter of Lord Winchelsea, when she ventured to

* Arbuthnot to Swift, July 15, 1714.

† Harrop's 'Bolingbroke,' p. 44.

tap him with her fan, a liberty which a previous consort, although a Percy, never dared to take.* He was father-in-law to Sir William Wyndham, and resented the accusation of complicity in the Rebellion of 1715, which was brought against that politician.

The second opponent who barred Bolingbroke's path was John, second Duke of Argyll. A soldier of considerable experience, he had been promoted by William the Third to command of a regiment when only nineteen, and subsequently served under the Duke of Marlborough at Ramillies, Oudenarde, and Malplaquet; but he was strangely jealous of his great commander's military renown. Subsequently Argyll was placed in command in Spain after Stanhope's defeat at Brihuega in 1710, and, failing to retrieve the English fortunes, believed that he had not been properly supported by Oxford and Bolingbroke, who were then negotiating the Treaty of Utrecht.†

The great Scotch magnate had the gift of oratory, and filled a leading position amongst the statesmen of George the First and George the Second.

As the Commander of the Forces in Scotland under the new Sovereign, the Duke of Argyll was soon to be called on to display such military skill as he

* Burnet's 'History of his own Times,' edition 1838, p. 732. In the year 1726, when sixty-five years of age, this Duke of Somerset, again a widower, became enamoured of the famous Duchess of Marlborough, but for once received a social rebuff himself, being told "if he was Emperor of the world she would not permit him to succeed to the heart which had been devoted to John Duke of Marlborough."—Alison's 'Marlborough,' vol. ii. p. 320.

† Coxe's 'Walpole,' vol. i. pp. 610, 611.

possessed, and meantime his best endeavours were given to support the Whig Government formed on the ruins of Bolingbroke's half-constructed Tory edifice.

And thus it happened that matters progressed smoothly towards the consummation then devoutly desired by the more solid portion of the English people, and since acknowledged as a blessing to civilization by generations who have tasted the sweets of liberty under the Guelphic rule.

The Privy Council appointed twenty-five Regents, including seven great Officers of State, and eighteen Lord Justices, the latter named by the new King, through Kreyenberg, directly Queen Anne died. That several of the former were not Whigs the following names will show: Dr. Tenison, Archbishop of Canterbury; Lord Chancellor Harcourt; John Sheffield, Duke of Buckingham, Lord President; Charles Talbot, Duke of Shrewsbury, Lord Treasurer; William Legg, Earl of Dartmouth, Lord Privy Seal; Thomas Wentworth, Earl of Strafford, First Commissioner of the Admiralty; and Sir Thomas Parker, Lord Justice of the King's Bench.

Moreover, a proclamation, styling George, Elector of Brunswick-Luneburg, King of Great Britain, France and Ireland, immediately received the signatures of more than one hundred lords and gentlemen, some of whom were destined to shed their blood for James Edward in a year's time, while Lord Isla, Argyll's brother, Lord Justice of North Britain, persuading his countrymen that Royal Stuart blood ran in George the First's veins, conducted the initial proceedings of proclaiming the new King with an *éclat* worthy of the Scotch nation, and of the beautiful capital city in which the ceremony was held.

In the Museum in Princes Street, Edinburgh, exposed on a screen for public view, may now be read the signatures of those who, on the ground we have indicated, welcomed George Lewis's representative to the ancient halls of Holyrood. Nor is it unworthy of record that prominent amongst the list of Highland chieftains and Lowland lairds was the name of Cameron of Lochiel. For in truth men looked forward wistfully to a truce of parties, during which, if many regrets were buried, decent sepulture was afforded them on the score that national unity was a necessity when law and order demanded some sacrifice from the partisan, on whatever side ranged.

A similar success having attended the formalities at Dublin, those responsible for the peace of England strained their attention in order to learn tidings of the Pretender's movements, and, above all, longed for King George's arrival.

In the meantime Bolingbroke's late endeavours to arm the ports having been left incomplete,*

* Lord Bolingbroke has been freely blamed for not having fortified the ports. We found this letter in his own handwriting, however, at the Record Office, which should be perused in justice to the statesman whose conduct has been so severely animadverted on:—

"Whitehall, May 25, 1714.

"Gentlemen,—As to the fortifications of Great Britain and the state of the stores there, and the necessary measures for proceeding on one, and for measures of defence were resolved on by the Regency, who chose the illustrious Addison to act as Secretary, and ignored Lord Bolingbroke contemptuously, obliging him to stand at the Council Chamber door with the very papers which had previously been addressed to him as Minister, while he was called on to receive peremptory orders from those who but yesterday were adjudged to be his subordinates. Moreover, the very first tidings from the King at Hanover contained an order to formally dismiss the late Secretary of State with contumely, similar to that which he had previously experienced at the hands of George the First's agents. If it is in the nature of a worm to turn, how much more likely is the lion to rend small creatures who conspire to disable him? and it is difficult to conceive an optimist capable of believing that, spurned from the Palace door, and crushed by his political enemies, a man of unsettled opinions and high spirit such as Bolingbroke would be slow to recognise and nurture the fast-growing reaction in favour of old-world ideas as represented by James Edward Stuart, which was threatening to embarrass the lately-crowned King of England.

---

replenishing the other, their Lordships will meet at my office to-morrow between six and seven in the evening, at which hour you will please attend them.

"I am, &c.,

"BOLINGBROKE.

"Principal Officers of; and Board of Ordnance."

There was clearly no wilful neglect on the Minister's part.

Much as this policy of the Hanoverian Whig leaders may be reprobated, it is not amazing to those who have become familiar with that remarkable collection of letters in the Hanover Papers which deal with this period. Kreyenberg, Bothmar, and Robethon are at one in the resolve to elevate the Whigs, and correspondingly depress the Tories. If the Elector caught the prevailing sentiment, it only survives in his alleged remark, when on starting for England he was reminded by a German friend of Charles the First's fate—"But the King-killers are all on my side."

Having committed the government of his German dominions to a Council under his brother Ernest, George the First embarked at Orange Polder on September 16, accompanied by Baron Bernsdorff, M. de Robethon, Count Platen, the Baron de Rhedo, the Marquess de la Foret, and (in spite of their having been disavowed in the Electoral Prince matter) the Baron Schutz and his two sons, together with a large *entourage* of foreigners.

The above-mentioned yacht *Peregrine*, and the *Mary*, were the Royal vessels which, accompanied by British and Dutch men-of-war, conveyed the new King and his suite to England. They reached the Thames in a fog, and so had to wait several hours before proceeding up the river to Greenwich, which the King reached at six o'clock in the evening of September 18, 1714. He took up his abode in the ancient palace erected by Edward the First, and specially connected with the Tudor dynasty, inasmuch as therein was born Henry the Eighth, while his two daughters Mary and Elizabeth also first saw light there.

After a triumphal entry into London with his son, the Prince of Wales, George the First was crowned at Westminster on October 20, 1714, with great magnificence—both Oxford and Bolingbroke being present; and in London the people received the King with enthusiasm, although in certain provincial districts, as we shall show, ominous discontent shortly disclosed itself.

The King, on his arrival in London, took up his residence at St. James's Palace. According to Rapin, the historian, he reached the metropolis on a bright and cool September day. On the following morning he was much surprised when, after gazing at the ornamental water in the park, he received a present of two fine carp from the ranger, Lord Chetwynd, and was told to give five guineas to the bearer for—as the King phrased it—"bringing me *my own* carp out of *my own* canal in *my own* park."* For so he had been led to regard St. James's Palace, and what was then its beautiful demesne.

Although the new King's wit can scarcely be described as of the highest order, yet he was an amusing companion after dinner, and many good-natured anecdotes are told of him which scarcely bear repetition. But it is right to record that George the

* Jesse's 'Court of England,' vol. ii. p. 306.

First, avowedly and constitutionally leaving to responsible Ministers questions of public policy, whether connected with the stability of his own dynasty or the direction of foreign affairs, as well as matters of trade and finance, yet ever displayed a commendable liberality of feeling towards the exiled claimants to his throne.

For instance, he retained the friendship of an old companion, who, although ready to smoke with him as of yore, would never salute him as King of Great Britain. Again, to a lady in a domino who, presumably at a masked ball, asked him to drink to the Pretender, he replied:

"I will drink with all my heart to the memory of any unfortunate prince."

Probably, however, the answer he gave to a German nobleman with whom he stayed on one of his journeys to Hanover, will be thought the most creditable of all the anecdotes recorded by that pleasant chronicler, Mr. John Heneage Jesse. Seeing a portrait, apparently of an English sovereign in full regal robes, George the First asked who it represented, and was told diffidently that the Chevalier de St. George had sent the picture to the owner, an acquaintance made at Rome:—

"Upon my word," said the King, "it is very like the family."

No greater delicacy of feeling, alike towards his unfortunate kinsman and the embarrassed host, could possibly be imagined.*

* Jesse's 'Court of England,' vol. ii. p. 309.

Lady Mary Wortley Montagu has left a vivid picture of the Court of St. James's early in this reign. Mr. Wortley being a Lord of the Treasury, his beautiful and witty wife was welcomed at a Court where many other possessors of such charming qualities declined to appear, such was the devotion of the old English families to the Stuarts. But not only did the King and the Duchess of Kendal,* who headed his table, become enchained by Lady Mary's beauty, but the susceptible Prince of Wales admired her also, although attendance at the levées of St. James's was usually by no means an *entrée* to Leicester House, the Heir-Apparent's residence.

One evening, Lady Mary, wishing to escape from a Royal party, found the admiring monarch loth to allow her to depart, which she nevertheless did, amidst many deprecatory but complimentary remarks. Unfortunately, however, she retailed her experiences to Mr. Secretary Craggs, whom she met in the courtyard at St. James's, and he, wishing to please George the First, carried Lady Mary upstairs in his arms, and deposited the fair burden close to that monarch, who was extremely delighted, exclaiming, "Ah! la revoila." However, Lady Mary, quite put off her guard, in her confusion exclaimed:

"Oh Lord, Sir, I have been so frightened,"

and then told the story just as she would have told

* The Duchess of Kendal was George the First's wife by a left-handed marriage. The Electress Sophia called her a Maukin, and wondered at her son's infatuation for her.—Coxe's 'Walpole,' vol. i. p. 82.

it to a subject. The Sovereign, much amused, asked Craggs if it was an English custom to carry ladies about like sacks of wheat, and was told in reply that it was done for His Majesty's satisfaction. Mr. Craggs' lame answer passed tolerably well, but he revenged himself on the tell-tale beauty by oaths and reproaches, which, to use her own words, she "durst not resent." *

There is no portion of West-end London more rich in interesting memories of the seventeenth and eighteenth centuries than those which cluster around the courtyard of that circumscribed Royal palace at St. James's, whence the Court of England is, in diplomatic parlance, supposed to issue its mandates. The spot is equally associated with the unfortunate Stuarts and with their Guelph successors. There the Prince Palatine was welcomed to the English Court by King James the First, although the Queen Anne of Denmark never could reconcile herself to what she deemed an unequal marriage with a pseudo prince, and hesitated to allow her beautiful daughter Elizabeth to leave for Germany. There the ill-fated James Edward first saw the light, and under that roof dwelt George the First.

* Lady M. W. Montagu's Works, vol. i. p. 38.

CHAPTER XII.

THE REBELLION OF 1715 AND ITS CAUSES.

THE rising which King George the First is believed to have apprehended before he left Hanover was only deferred, not prevented, and, as will be shown, the Brunswick-Luneburg family were speedily compelled to wrestle with what threatened to become a desperate situation. But the Fates fought for them, and quickly averted the imminent disaster.

A candid family friend—and they would doubtless have been forthcoming in numbers had defeat and abdication awaited the new King—might plausibly have ascribed his downfall to the questionable policy of propitiating only one of the great parties which had, on the whole, fairly shared power since the Revolution of 1688. Dr. Sacheverell was at Sutton, near Birmingham, about this time, and employed his time in vigorously preaching, in and out of the pulpit, against the threatened Whig domination. As a consequence, excited mobs arose at Birmingham, dispersing by force a loyal gathering which had assembled to celebrate the Coronation.* In Stafford-

* Rapin's 'History of England,' vol. xviii. p. 327.

shire excited crowds attacked the Dissenting meeting-houses, necessitating the reading of a stringent Riot Act passed through Parliament with haste for the purpose.* Similar disorders, moreover, occurred at Bristol, Chippenham, Norwich and Reading. On the other hand, it is fair to add that many formal addresses of loyalty reached St. James's from other parts of the kingdom, while Cambridge University spoke strongly out for the Brunswick *régime.*

The King had brought over with him, in lieu of the unfortunate Sophia Dorothea of Celle, who was still immured in Ahlen Castle, two female companions, one of whom, the Duchess of Kendal, has already been mentioned. The other was the Countess Platen. The German *entourage,* male and female, became exceedingly unpopular, and it is said to have been one of the latter who, when execrated by the people, thrust her head out of the window and cried, in broken English, "My friends, we are come for your goots;" some British wag rejoining, "Aye, and for our chattels too." Cries of "Ormond" and "High Church for ever!" were frequent among the people at this time, even in London, where the Whig commercial class generally, no doubt, were for the Protestant Succession; but the cry of "Down with the Hanover rats!" was frequently raised;† while more serious still, the British Guards were discontented, nominally at the quality of their clothes,

* 'History of Europe from the Peace of Utrecht,' by Lord John Russell, Book ii. p. 3.

† Coxe's 'Life of Marlborough,' vol. vi. p. 318.

Marlborough finding it necessary to ply them well with beer before even he could bring them into a contented state of mind.*

The violent party spirit displayed by the triumphant Whigs had doubtless raised this alarming ferment. The leaders of the late Ministry, Oxford and Bolingbroke, were impeached on the charge of high treason for collusion with the late Queen's enemies; Walpole and his political associates undertaking, in effect, to show that there was a settled resolve to bring back the Pretender.

The Tory party, broken to pieces, made but little open resistance, while circumstances were conspiring to tempt the doubting section of that party into the purely Jacobite ranks. Who, for instance, believes Sir William Wyndham had any natural inclination in that direction? Lord Bolingbroke, as is well known, did not await the risks of a trial. He felt sure that those of his enemies who were in power, and therefore able to compass his destruction, had determined to take the life they held forfeit for the manner in which its owner concluded the Treaty of Utrecht, and for the alleged design, attributed to him by these unrelenting detractors, of forcing the Pretender upon this country in defiance of law and without regard to liberty. He fled without even waiting for the attainder, and in contravention of his assurances to Lord Stair, the English Ambassador at Paris, joined the Pretender. It is said that the

* Coxe's 'Life of Marlborough,' vol. vi. p. 319.

Duke of Marlborough had warned Bolingbroke not to await the decision of a tribunal called together to register the adverse decision of his enemies, probably to condemn him to death, and that he retreated to France in consequence.

Lord Oxford, on the other hand, never quailed before the tempest roused by his political foes, and, conscious that the case against him could not be proved, he comported himself with manifest dignity, being taken to the Tower amidst varying expressions of popular opinion. In this enforced retirement he employed his leisure in inditing from time to time letters in the Latin language, so that the warders might not understand them.* Amongst these epistles was one, indited during a moment of resentment, which engaged the writer to assist the Pretender.

It was impossible that the country gentlemen of England as a class, together with nearly all the learned clergy in the country, should be denied a just share in the Government, and yet that leaders, such as Bolingbroke and Oxford, should still remain faithful to a new *régime* which professed to desire their degradation and death, and really did intend to exclude them, together with those they represented, from power.†

It has been generally assumed that the danger to

* The 'Welbeck Papers' contain most of these communications. They are to be catalogued and arranged at the Record Office.

† That great Whig magnate, the late Earl Russell, has left on record that his party were goaded to resentment because of "glory missed" in 1710–11.—'History of Europe from the Peace of Utrecht,' vol. i. p. 335.

the Brunswick dynasty was greater in 1708 and 1745, and fraught with more danger in 1718 and 1719, when the Pretender was at Madrid under Cardinal Alberoni's protection, than in 1715, because on the latter occasion England was at peace. The death of Louis the Fourteenth in this eventful year, 1715, rendered any renewed hostility from France improbable, and so deprived the Jacobites of their great family general, the Duke of Berwick, whose presence in Scotland would probably have altered the course of events. For in spite of the fact that Lord Mar's precipitate counsels caused the struggle to be practically concluded before the Pretender reached Peterhead, near Aberdeen, yet there is reason to believe that a prompt and resolute advance might have carried all before it in Scotland, while the conflict in England would then have been determined under totally different conditions. For the people were undoubtedly less favourable to the Brunswick family in 1715 than at any other period during which their rule was in question; while, most portentous fact of all! Marlborough had sent the Pretender a sum of money to defray the charges of his expedition,* and yet nominally directed George the First's military affairs. Even when instead of—as in Berwick's opinion he ought to have done—pushing on to Stirling and Edinburgh with his whole force, Mar remained

* Lord Stanhope's 'History of England from the Peace of Utrecht,' vol. i. Appendix, p. 33, 4th edition.

inactive at Perth, the danger to the Protestant dynasty was still very real. Detached from the main Jacobite body, Colonel Macintosh, with two thousand picked Highlanders, joined hands on the Tweed, at Kelso, with Lord Kenmure, who had raised the southern counties of Galloway and Dumfries. Argyll was thus placed between two fires, while in the northern counties of England an insurrection smouldered, such as, had it not been promptly suppressed when it burst forth prematurely, must have brought about the conditions which Marlborough expected and was prepared to recognise. Lancashire was undoubtedly ready to rise, and a single success would have brought thousands to the Jacobite standard. However, when Mr. Forster and Lord Derwentwater, with 1400 men, were surrounded at Preston and forced to surrender, the rebellion became isolated in Scotland, and so lost its sting. For Ormond had failed to arouse the west, and the Highlanders of Macintosh, shrinking from crossing the border, had left the deluded insurgents of Cumberland, Northumberland, and Lancashire to their fate.

These events occurred in November, 1715, so that it was not until the 13th of December that Mar fought the celebrated and indecisive battle of Sheriffmuir, near Dunblane. "Oh for one hour of Dundee!" is said to have been the cry of Gordon of Glenbucket, an old Killiecrankie man, during the first *mêlée* of the clans, when but for a Dutch contingent which succoured Argyll, the Jacobite, Highlanders would have outnumbered their loyal countrymen from Argyleshire.

A week after this event, and when the insurrection had already spent its force in England, while it languished in Scotland, James Edward, to use his own words, appeared in his ancient kingdom.* How, disguised as a naval officer, he passed from Peterhead through Feteresso to Perth, and thence to Scone, and designed his coronation there in January, 1716, is well known. How also, when Mar retreated a month afterwards, the Pretender—for we can henceforth give him no other name even in Scotland—escaped to Montrose, and embarked for France, February 4, 1716, is likewise familiar to every one who has read the history of his country, On the other hand, probably few have gauged the immensity of the peril from which this nation was then delivered.

Had Lord Bolingbroke—still on friendly terms with Marlborough—been allowed to shape the course of the rebellion from his Parisian hiding-place, there is little doubt that the outbreak would not have consisted of isolated explosions, the smoke of which James Edward was called in to view when there was no more powder available. Therefore it is that we regard the subsequent attempts to overthrow the

* While Lord Stanhope's and other accounts of this rebellion have been consulted, we owe much to the late Sir Archibald Alison's 'Marlborough,' vol. ii. pp. 273–286. Sir Archibald knew the country, and was in the habit of visiting every battlefield he described.

Brunswick dynasty as of minor importance. Englishmen, for instance, would never have permanently agreed to accept a king at Spanish dictation, because Cardinal Alberoni had revived the resources of that country in 1717. Nor is it possible to believe that if the persevering Ormond had not been driven from Scotland in 1719 by the adverse elements, his presence would have saved from capture the handful of Spaniards who then surrendered near that lovely spot between Arisaig and Fort William yclept Glenfinnan, where Charles Edward's standard was first set up in 1745. As for the threatened rebellion of 1722, which brought about the discovery of Atterbury's treason, this danger happily arose when Bolingbroke was constrained by reason of his pardon to remain at least neutral, and when Marlborough had really resolved to throw his influence into supporting the Brunswick cause.

The Jacobites seem to have been lured on from day to day by confident belief in a Restoration, and Mary of Modena's own statement to the Abbess of Chaillot proves this. She says: "When I first passed over to France, if any one had told me I should have to remain here two years, I should have been in despair, and I have been upwards of two and twenty." * On the other hand, the Stuart papers at Windsor concerning Atterbury, which Mr. J. H. Glover edited, show † how active the eloquent bishop

* Miss Strickland's 'Princesses of the House of Stuart,' p. 362.

† See p. 18, also p. 130, where an attempt to re-enlist Bolingbroke is mentioned.

had been even before his historic trial and able defence, the adverse result of which compelled him to make Paris the base of his secret operations against George the First. Nor is it possible to ignore the fact that between the years 1722–24 the Scotch Episcopal Bishops were elected by the Pretender's direct orders.* In England the clergy, led by Bishop Atterbury and Dr. Snape, Head-master of Eton, pressed the doctrine of non-resistance in 1717 to its logical conclusion, and raised such a tempest—known as the Bangorian controversy—that Convocation was suspended, never to meet again until 1854, under Lord Aberdeen's administration.

We revert to Alberoni's projects for the purpose of calling attention to a very interesting document preserved in the Hanover Papers, that magazine of eighteenth-century history. A few introductory remarks are necessary. One of the first things Cardinal Alberoni did on gaining supreme power in Spain, was to take the Chevalier de St. George under his protection, as a means of strengthening himself against England, and detaching France, if possible, from the triple alliance which that nation had formed with England and Holland. However, without proclaiming war, the English Government sent Sir George Byng into that part of the Mediterranean where the Spanish fleet had been ordered to rendezvous.

The British Admiral found them off Messina, and

* 'Lockhart Papers,' vol. ii. p. 23.

an action ensued, in which the English fleet, carrying 1400 guns, nearly destroyed the Spanish, with only 1284 guns, one wing alone escaping to Malta under Admiral George Cammock, who was acting under the Pretender's orders.* Byng received a letter from Cammock, calling on him to take his fleet into Messina and, joining with that of Spain, sail towards England. This letter, after threatening him with divers penalties ordained of God and St. Paul, on the ground "that whosoever resisteth the ordinance shall receive to himself Damnation," goes on, "a death-bed repentance will avail but little, for without Restitution repentance availeth nothing." He must therefore restore the Pretender, whose appearance and character he thus describes:—

"As England has now at this time only a Cypher of a King and a sham pretending Prince of Wales, now Sir George give me leave to lay before you and that with truth the true character of yours and mine lawful master whom God preserve.

"He is tall, slender, comely, the upper part of his face very much like Charles II.,† the lower part very much like the late Queen Mother, sharp, quick, Eye very perceptable, his Judgment extremely good on all subjects that are talked on.

"He speaks as good English as if he had had his Education in England, he is well acquainted with the Laws of his Country and perfectly with Clarendon's History and the manners of the people of England, whenever he talks of his Subjects it is with great compassion and affection for his poor deluded people. As to his natural dispositions he is affable, Courteous, kind, generous,

* Mahon's 'History of England,' vol. i. p. 315.

† There must have been some truth in this likeness, for Mr. Leslie, the well-known Non-juror, describes the Chevalier as tall and active in his person, resembling Charles the Second in countenance.—Lord Russell's 'History of the Peace of Utrecht,' Bk. ii. ch. i. p. 6.

brave, and of a forgiving temper, he has no desire of revenge to his worst of enemies on the contrary, for I have had the honour to hear him say at his table to the Duke of Ormond that he would forgive even Marlborough, Sunderland, Townsend and Stanhope, his greatest enemies if it should please God to restore him."

Admiral Cammock proceeds to set forth the main object of his letter, and offers bribes all round if Sir George will only embrace the project in question:—

"The King commands me to tell you that if you will bring into Messina or any port of Spain the majority of your fleet, so that it may be capable in conjunction with the Spanish fleet to beat the remainder of the Usurper's fleet, that he will reward you with the same title as General Monk had for the restoring Charles II. And for the better maintaining the honour and dignity of Duke of Albemarle, his Majesty will give you one hundred thousand pounds sterling as his royal bounty, for which security the King of Spain will be guaranty, and furthermore First Lord of the Admiralty, or Admiral Commander and chief of his Majesty's fleet, which of those two you will make choice of."

Cammock goes on to promise each captain of the fleet who complies 10,000*l.* sterling, making him also knight of a newly created order. As to the subaltern officers, they who gave proof of loyalty were to be preferred according to merit. Able seamen and soldiers, on the other hand, were to be paid all arrears of wages due to them during the time they served the so-called usurping King, George the First.*

* We quote from a summary of Cammock's letter, which the author of this work contributed in October 1885 to the 'English Historical Review,' taken straight from the Hanover Papers.

This remarkable statement concludes, as it commenced, with mingled adulation and threatening. It is dated October 14, 1718, and was apparently withheld until the general action off Messina which resulted so disastrously for Spain. Cammock, escaping with his wing of the fleet, added a postscript at Valetta. This disaster, although it by no means appalled Alberoni, weakened Spain on the sea, while the death of the Swedish king, Charles the Twelfth, made one enemy less to England and the Protestant Succession. Ultimately all efforts to break up the alliance between France and England having failed, Alberoni's bold projects collapsed, and he was sent back to Italy.

Our task is practically finished when a date is reached after which due consideration makes it possible to declare that the Guelph family remained secure upon that throne they have rendered so famous. There remains, therefore, but to sum up shortly what have been the constitutional influences which have attended their elevation. Of course this security was really brought about by Walpole; although it is well to correct an error frequently made, to the effect that this great financier became the First Minister of George the First, whereas his elevation did not take place until after Townsend, Stanhope, and Sunderland had severally occupied the post. He was then placed in power, because the national finance was completely broken down by the bursting of the South Sea Bubble. It is true that the Septennial Act was really initiated by this pre-eminent Whig leader, but Lord Townsend was nevertheless Minister at the time; while the Tripartite Treaty which united France, England and Holland, was owing to the diplomatic sagacity of Stanhope and Sunderland, which defeated for the nonce that tendency of France and Spain to unite adversely to English interests which Professor Seeley has detected and fixed, as we think unfairly, upon the Treaty of Utrecht and its designers.

Before bringing this chapter to a conclusion by mentioning the dangers which threatened the person of our first Guelphic King, we transcribe Horace Walpole's striking picture of his father's Royal master:—

"I must suppose," he says, "that the female attendants in the family must have put it into my head to long to see the King. This childish caprice was so strong, that my mother solicited the Duchess of Kendal to obtain for me the honour of kissing his Majesty's hand before he set out for Hanover. A favour so unusual to be asked for a boy of ten years old, was still too slight to be refused to the wife of the First Minister for her darling child; yet not being proper to be made a precedent, it was settled to be in private and at night.

"Accordingly, the night but one before the King began his last journey, my mother carried me at 10 at night, to the apartment of the Countess of Walsingham, on the ground floor towards the garden of St. James, which opened into that of her aunt the Duchess of Kendal; apartments occupied by George the Second after his Queen's death, and by his successive mistresses the Countesses of Suffolk and Yarmouth. Notice being given that the King was come down to supper, Lady Walsingham took me alone into the Duchess's ante-room, where we found the King and her.

"I knelt down and kissed his hand. He said a few words to me, and my conductress led me back to my mother.

"The person of the King is as perfect in my memory as if I saw him but yesterday. It was that of an elderly man, rather pale, and exactly like his pictures and coins; not tall, of an aspect rather good than august, with a dark tie wig, a plain coat, waistcoat, and breeches of snuff-coloured cloth, with stockings of the same colour, and a blue riband over all.

"So entirely was he my object, that I do not believe I looked once at the Duchess; but as I could not avoid seeing her on entering the room I remember that just beyond his Majesty stood a very tall, lean, ill-favoured old lady; but I did not retain the least idea of her features, nor know what the colour of her dress was."

Walpole records in another place that the King took him in his arms, kissed him, and chatted some time. It is remarkable that notwithstanding the fierce religious political controversies which raged over the question of the Succession, once only was the life of George the First endangered from assassination. A fanatic boy of eighteen, James Shepherd, apprentice to a coachmaker, did meditate the death of the King in 1718; not that with the Prince of Wales alive the youthful regicide could hope to gain his end, and make way for the exiled Stuarts. However, refusing to express the slightest contrition or sorrow for his intended crime, Shepherd was hanged at Tyburn in March of the same year.*

George the First was in great danger of shipwreck on his return from Hanover in 1726, inasmuch as his vessel was caught in a violent storm, and after

* Jesse's 'Court of England,' vol. ii. p. 304.

beating about for two days in the Channel, he was with difficulty landed at Rye, in Sussex.* This did not, however, prevent him from setting out on the final journey to his Electorate during the ensuing year 1727, when he died on the road to Osnaburg, June 11, aged 68.

* 'Lives of Eminent Englishmen,' 1838, vol. iv. p. 16.

CHAPTER XIII.

THE LATER GUELPHS.

A.D. 1727–1887.

Sir Robert Walpole, the Premier, conscious that a coalition of parties assailed him, expected that he would be called upon to make room for Sir Spencer Compton on the King's demise. That George the Second preferred in the first days of his reign to retain his father's faithful servant in office was due to the intervention of that wonderful woman Queen Caroline, who had heard the late King say, when threatened with an apparent financial necessity for disbanding the Hanoverian troops,—"No, for Walpole can convert stones into gold." Impressing this fact upon her husband while representing the extraordinarily wide scope of Walpole's genius for government, the Queen bade fair to carry her point, when her womanly wit led her to suggest casually, as it were, that Sir Robert intended to augment the Civil List to the amount of £130,000. This consideration seems to have decided the battle, and with Walpole once more supreme at Whitehall, the barrier to Jacobite advance was strengthened at the critical moment.*

Compton had actually received an offer of the Premiership from the King, and had shed tears as he avowed his incapacity to undertake the office. Little did he think that the Queen had divined the situation so completely that she would speedily persuade her husband that his throne depended on retaining Walpole in power. It is said that Sir Robert, passing through St. James's Square at this moment, saw Compton's house besieged by persons of all ranks anxious to pay court to the new Minister, whereupon Sir Robert remarked, "My house is deserted, and how that door is crowded with carriages! It will be different to-morrow." †

The nation is still reaping the advantage which accrued from Queen Caroline's sagacious interposition. Under the guidance of a Minister endowed with remarkable breadth of view and foresight, the course of policy pursued in George the Second's reign tended to render the government of Great Britain more popular, and by consequence more stable. Up to this point the account of the progress of the Brunswick dynasty has concerned us with the actions of sovereigns, princes, and their personal advisers, seeing that even the events which were most inspired by the popular will, took shape and

* Coxe's 'Walpole,' vol. i. pp. 285, 286.

† Ibid., p. 287.

colour from the characters and actions of such exalted individuals. But the strength of the throne tenanted by George the First and his son was based on a popular desire to preserve a rational form of monarchical government in the interests of personal freedom and social order. These national blessings were both threatened by the danger of a Jacobite restoration which would have involved the entrance of the Jesuits from St. Germain on the political stage of Great Britain.

Walpole had therefore one leading object in view when he strove to propitiate France at almost any hazard, and preserved peace under circumstances which men believed calculated to injure English influence abroad if the nation remained inactive. He was resolved to provide no haven for the Pretender near our own shores. This policy succeeded so well, that despite the inevitable rustiness of the defences both by sea and land, which ensued upon neglect of military and naval preparation, the resources of the country were husbanded, and her finance placed upon a scientific basis. Urged by that able adviser Mr. Arthur Moore, who supported Walpole as fervently as he formerly had stood by Bolingbroke, the policy initiated when framing the Treaty of Utrecht, became that of the great Whig party in their hour of triumph. In the matter of Foreign Policy, however, it is impossible to believe that had Sir Robert Walpole, or his able diplomatic coadjutor and brother Horatio

Walpole,* together with Mr. Arthur Moore, been unshackled, they would ever have pursued the line which they elected almost continuously to follow, until at last public excitement forced them into the war known as that "of Jenkins' ear," † which commenced in October 1739. It was in reality a struggle for the trade of South America, and—oh! shades of Wilberforce and Clarkson!—one waged to retain a monopoly in the slave traffic which disgraced those regions.

Popular in its inception, this war was welcomed by the people with ringing of bells, on hearing which Walpole remarked, "they will soon be wringing their hands;" and well might that remark have proved true if Spain had possessed her former strength; but, despite the English unpreparedness which soon became notorious, the Walpole Administration got more respectably out of their difficulties than, under the circumstances, they had any right to expect.

* It is necessary, for the sake of those unfamiliar with this period, to distinguish between Sir Robert's brother, the diplomatist, and his younger son Horace, the brilliant letter writer and literary character. Mr. Speaker Onslow says regarding Mr. Arthur Moore: "Mr. Moore had very extraordinary talents, with great experience and knowledge of the world, very able in Parliament and capable of the highest parts of business, with a manner in it, and indeed in his general deportment, equal almost to any rank. He knew everybody, and could talk of everybody, which made his conversation a sort of history of the age.

"He was generous and magnificent; wrote and spoke accurately and politely; but his figure was awkward and disadvantageous."—Burnet's 'History of his own Times,' edition 1838, p. 898.

† A certain English captain, Jenkins by name, was said to have been half-hanged at the yard-arm by some Spaniards, who then cut off his ear. The story is a very doubtful one.

Porto Bello, on the Isthmus of Panama, was taken, and mysterious signboards in remote portions of England commemorate the victory in question to this day.* Drifting on languidly and without definite result, this contest between England and Spain continued until the peace of Aix-la-Chapelle in 1748, before which the war of the Austrian Succession had given fresh hopes to the Stuart exiles at Rome. The Emperor Charles the Sixth, who had been the cause of the last European war when Imperial candidate for the throne of Spain, left his hereditary dominions in Austria and Hungary to his daughter Maria Theresa, and so in his death brought about another continental struggle, because the King of Spain and the Duke of Bavaria preferred claims which it suited Frederick the Great to second indirectly by invading Silesia. George the Second had given his word to the late Emperor Charles the Sixth to support the so-called Pragmatic Sanction which was designed to retain the throne for Maria Theresa, and straightway England and Walpole were dragged into the general fray. With a condition of war ceased Walpole's usefulness—indeed his very *raison d'être*, as to guarding the Succession soon to be again threatened when France was once more in the field as England's enemy. A vote of the House of Commons in 1742 put a seal upon what had been long evident, viz. that Walpole was, owing to the

* What hunting-man has not at some time or other gruelled his horse at some hostel of the name?

direction of his ends and aims, no War Minister. He stands, it is true, probably second to none who have ruled England in the science of government, although mixed with the pure gold of his domestic statesmanship was the alloy of borough corruption, the latter being part of the price paid for our liberty, the remaining portion of which was the unreadiness for war associated with the policy of retrenchment then in vogue.

When peace ceased and Walpole's useful career closed, the English had the satisfaction of contemplating the gallantry of their King at Dettingen in 1743, the campaign on the Main resulting favourably for Maria Theresa. Handel, as is well known, celebrated the event in his celebrated *Te Deum*, and but for the advent of Marshal Saxe on the scene, the truthful historian might still have told of unchequered British triumph in the field. For Dettingen, despite its comparative inutility, may be so classed.

This celebrated hireling—for he was really Count Maurice of Saxe, and no Frenchman—was destined to undo all Marlborough's work, and inflict defeat after defeat upon the English on the Flemish frontier, starting from a base of operation whence the former victories and sacrifices of Great Britain should have precluded her from being assailed. We read then in the triumphant advance of Marshal Saxe in 1745 a condemnation of the premature haste in which the frontier was settled at Utrecht in 1712, and with these facts before his eyes Bolingbroke made his famous apologies to Sir William Wyndham, when he acknowledged that France was too leniently treated in 1713. The battle of Fontenoy left the fortress of Tournay in French hands, while it is mere pinchbeck patriotism which seeks to obscure the fact, that stubbornly as the English fought, they came off second best on that occasion. Led by the Duke of Cumberland, a youth of 24, the English were separated from their Austro-Dutch allies at the critical moment of this battle, after one of the most desperate charges recorded in military history.*

It followed as a matter of course that the Stuarts would make some effort to regain the English throne when they saw "Dapper George," as the British King was called, involved in a losing struggle with France, Prussia, and Spain.

It is a remarkable fact that Sir Robert Walpole, who foresaw, and strove to prevent such a conjuncture of affairs as had arrived, died in March, 1745, while in May came Fontenoy.

Before three months had ensued, James Edward's son, Charles Edward, then twenty-five years old, full of energy and enthusiasm, had landed in Scotland. He had been sent for from Rome by the French Ministry, which had arrived at a resolution to invade England—Marshal Saxe and 15,000 men being

* We owe this account of the military situation to Morris's 'Early Hanoverians,' from whose pleasant pages much may be learnt by those who have not leisure for consulting longer histories.

destined to escort the young prince to his father's hereditary dominions.

Not only, however, did the English fleet put in what to Franco-Jacobite eyes must have seemed an unwelcome appearance, but the elements were adverse, as indeed they always have been when such expeditions were in progress.

We shall avoid here any description of the "45." It has occupied alike the pen of romance and historical description.

Charles Edward at Derby with his Highlanders, George the Second encamped at Finchley amidst his guards and the London train bands; the Duke of Cumberland at Lichfield, and General Wade two days' march behind on the track of Charles Edward. Such was the situation, out of which the late Lord Stanhope has deduced the opinion, that if instead of retreating back into Scotland the Highlanders had pressed on to the Metropolis, the Jacobite partisans would have risen to the occasion, and the Brunswick *régime* have *temporarily* come to a close.* It is reasonable to respect the opinion of a competent historian who had made the subject in question his special study, and so we leave the matter—thankful beyond all telling that the Highlanders did quarrel amongst themselves at Derby, for the alternative otherwise presented was at the very best of it no-

* Lord Stanhope argues that if the battle of Falkirk had been won near London, the Metropolis would have declared for the victors, and James Edward have been proclaimed King. But even then Wade and the Duke of Cumberland would have had to be reckoned with.

thing but renewed rebellion and civil war. For the principles which James the Second put in practice, and James Edward refused to desert, had been instilled into Charles Edward in Rome, and having drunk them in, so to speak, with his mother's milk, he would not have been likely either to influence his father in a contrary direction, or give parliamentary government free play when the Royal mantle should fall upon his own shoulders.

The more deeply the history of this period is studied and pondered over, the more will the day be blessed on which the bravery and chivalry of gallant Prince Charlie were relegated to the delightful region of Scotch romance, while the sceptre of England was still grasped by her Brunswick kings.

The insurrection of 1745 occurred during the so-called Broad Bottom Administration of the brothers Pelham—Sir Henry of that ilk, and the Duke of Newcastle, who, for a short period after the former moderate and high-minded Minister died, held the Premiership of England. But they were soon to be eclipsed by the magic power of a great mind, the qualities of which had enchanted the people of England.

Clearer in the style of oratory which he adopted than even his great predecessor, Bolingbroke, who had died in 1751,* the elder Pitt forced himself into power by the sheer force of genius, which he then straightway applied to the task of crippling France,

* See Appendix.

who in 1758 was committed to a struggle for empire all over the world with her ancient foe. The French were driven from Canada, and their hopes of supreme empire in the East Indies blasted, while the British flag floated triumphantly over the world. On the other hand, although the elder Pitt withdrew our armies from the Continent after the battle of Minden, fought in defence of Hanover in 1759, he subsidised Frederick the Great in his struggle with Russia, Saxony, Sweden, France, and the Empire, thus initiating a mode of waging war that the son availed himself of in the struggle with revolutionary France. And so it was that before that venerable sovereign George the Second, bereft of the counsel of the wife and the Minister on whom he had relied so long, died at the age of sixty-eight years, A.D. 1760, England was at last supreme in all four quarters of the globe.

George the Second fills no mean niche in the history of this nation; and his name has so often been mentioned here, both as Electoral Prince and King of England, that he cannot be dismissed without further comment.

There is an amusing story told of this King, how that, having been induced to witness a performance of Richard the Third by Garrick, he had his Royal fancy taken by the man who acted Lord Mayor, and, ignoring the great actor altogether, kept on repeating, "I like dat Lor Mayor; when will he come again."

The sober side of the King's somewhat incongruous character is seen at its best whenever his affection for Queen Caroline peeps out through the brusqueries and passionate outbursts which fill the pages of Lord Hervey's 'Memoirs.'

We would adduce two instances culled therefrom, namely, the letter full of tenderness and exquisite feeling which the King wrote to the spouse who ruled him, when in 1736 he had nearly lost his life at sea, between Holland and England,* and secondly, the words in which, after her death, he again disclosed the depth of the affection which enchained him.†

It is not generally known that he caused their dust to be mingled in death, the late Dean Milman when a Prebendary of Westminster having seen the stone sarcophagus which contained the two coffins, each of which lacked one side.‡

This appreciation of womanly influence in his family was further exemplified by an abiding affection for his unfortunate mother, Sophia Dorothea, whose picture, full length in royal robes, Lady Suffolk in her 'Memoirs' tells us was found both in the late Queen's dressing-room and in George the

* We give an excerpt from the original French, being anxious not to disturb the proportion of the King's feeling sentences:—

"Malgré tout le danger que j'ai essuié dans cette tempête, ma chère Caroline, et malgré tout ce que j'ai souffert, en étant malade à un point que je ne croiois pas que le corps humain pourroit souffrir, je vous jure que je m'exposerois encore et encore pour avoir le plaisir d'entendre les marques de votre tendresse que cette situation m'a procuré."—Lord Hervey's 'Memoirs,' edition 1884, vol. iii. p. 25.

† Lord Hervey's 'Memoirs,' vol. iii. p. 347.

‡ See note by the late J. W. Croker, ibid., pp. 347, 348.

Second's bed-chamber after his death. These portraits, we are told, he had till then kept concealed.*

His respect for women, and his being completely under Queen Caroline's influence, are quite enough to account for the mutual hatred which late in their lives existed between Frederick Prince of Wales and his parents, although an earlier dislike to this child of high destiny was evinced before the Electoral Prince and Princess had left Hanover. And this because, as Lord Hervey tells us, the Prince of Wales was a veritable woman-hater, and despised George the Second for his subjection to the Queen, of which the contemporary ballad speaks,

> "You may strut, dapper George, but 'twill all be in vain;
> We know 'tis Queen Caroline, not you, that reign—
> You govern no more than Don Philip of Spain."

Brave the King undoubtedly was, as his behaviour at Oudenarde, and afterwards at Dettingen, proved, while the above-mentioned danger of shipwreck, almost a replica of the peril undergone by his father in 1726, displayed this quality to great advantage. But then he was always boasting of this natural gift, and kept the softer side of his nature hidden from his subjects, and hence we prefer to dwell thereon. Shortly before his sudden death the Duchess of Hamilton, formerly the beautiful Miss Gunning, thoughtlessly said to the King in conversation, "there is only one other sight in the world which I should

* Lord Hervey's 'Memoirs,' vol. iii. p. 349, note by late J. W. Croker.

wish to behold, and that is a coronation." The King took her hand and added sadly, "you will soon have your desire."* The death of this venerable monarch, although sudden, was not unexpected.

The reign of George the Third saw the fusion of the various branches pertaining to the British Royal Family happily accomplished, when the events of the French Revolution caused Henry Stuart, Cardinal of York, the last of the eldest branch, to turn in dire need to his Royal kinsman at St. James's. And so when the said Cardinal died in 1807, all the crown jewels which James the Second took away from England were restored, and the family papers found their way to the King's library at Windsor, an acknowledgment that the Royal mantle had fallen on the owner of that ancient palace.

It is not possible to pass by the wonderful reign of George the Third without a few words about the three controverted points regarding the last forty years of the 18th century on which men debate energetically to this day, the historian scarcely daring to speak with certain sound regarding any one of them.

1. Did King George the Third and Lord North, without the support of a majority of the people, or indeed, as some have averred, guided only by their own stubborn wills, drive the American colonists into

* Cunningham's 'Lives of Eminent Englishmen,' Edition 1836, vol. v. p. 11.

rebellion; or had the people of England, as the late Earl Russell believed, act and part in that fell fiasco?

2. Did the younger Pitt, as Charles Fox, Lord Shelburne, and Lord Grey believed, and as a certain class of Whig writers and speakers still declare,* create Napoleon the First by not welcoming the principles of 1789, which under the attempt at international coercion became those of the Jacobins and reached a climax in 1793? Or was Lord Chatham's son, as George Canning thought, the British pilot "who weathered the storm?"

3. Finally—and the question is, alas! being *bitterly* debated even now—were the Ministry of 1799–1800 justified by the events of the Irish Rebellion, and the assumed dangers to England of threatened Hibernian dependence on foreign powers, in extinguishing the Protestant Parliamentary institution which Grattan had established in Dublin? Answers to questions such as these cannot be looked for in a summary dealing with a subject purely dynastic, but we look with interest for the verdict of a living writer, regarding the last two problems, seeing that Mr. Lecky, if he has ventured to express no very positive conclusions as to other controversial points submitted to his judgment, is yet thoroughly in touch with the last century and its stirring events.

Before taking a final glance at the personal influ-

* Mr. Bright has placed these views clearly before his countrymen, and they have been endorsed by Mr. Gladstone.

ence of the several Brunswick Sovereigns, it is necessary to notice shortly the Dukes of Brunswick proper, whose line came to an end in 1884. Ernest Duke of Celle, the friend of Luther, and common father of all the Anglo-German Guelphs, had a second son, Henry, who lived in retirement, but bequeathed his fortune, when he died in 1596, to his own child, Augustus Duke of Wolfenbüttel, who had similar tastes, although of a more pronouncedly literary character.

Nor did Augustus's successor, Ferdinand Albert the First, write his name in the roll of worldly fame. Then occurred a coincidence most uncommon in any family record.*

Three generations of the Ducal Brunswickers successively became famous as commanders in the field.

Ferdinand Albert the Second, disgusted with the spectacle of Hanover under the hoof of a French occupation, in which the convention of Closter-seven had forced the people to concur in 1757, rallied his countrymen to an assertion of their rights and liberties.

Encouraged by Frederick the Great's triumph at Rosbach, the gallant Brunswickers were equal to the occasion, proving in 1759, at the battle of Minden, that the spirit of Henry the Lion lingered amongst them. Hanover was thus cleared of the invader,

* Sir A. Halliday's 'House of Guelph,' pp. 115, 116.

who is believed to have escaped on terms greatly to his advantage.*

The next Duke of Brunswick is even more famous than his predecessor, because after learning the art of war under the great Frederick, it fell to Charles William Ferdinand's lot † to conduct the army of the first European Coalition against revolutionary France into the territories of that distressed country. The clash of arms took place at Valmy, in the north-east of France, on the 20th of September, 1792, when the world stood amazed to see the veteran hosts of Prussia arrested by the citizen levies of Gaul under Kellermann. The battle of Valmy was a wondrous event, but not so astounding as the subsequent retreat of the Prussians under their Brunswick leader, for at the very uttermost a serious check, and nothing beyond, can, from a military point of view, be registered as the direct result of Valmy. Its consequences, however, were stupendous when the general retired in consequence of secret orders from home, and military Europe confessed itself unable to execute a mandate against hastily summoned multitudes in France, the untrained champions of the

* Russell's 'Modern Europe,' Edition 1827, vol. ii. p. 471. There was a famous controversy between Lord George Sackville and Ferdinand of Brunswick regarding the inactivity of the troops led by the former.

† As Captain-General of Holland he sustained the cause of the Stadtholder William the Seventh against the Republican party during a minority of 15 years. Duke Charles William Ferdinand must have been the more moved by his failure to settle the internal affairs of France by force of arms in that during 1787 he had conducted a similar project successfully in the Low Countries, taking Amsterdam and defeating the Republicans.—'Annual Register,' 1787, p. 63.

Revolution. After an interval of seclusion, Duke Charles William Ferdinand again took the field in the year 1806, when on Oct. 4 he fell nobly at Auerstadt, and was happily saved from witnessing Prussia's period of agony.

The name of his son Frederick William, who died at the head of his Black Brunswickers at Quatre Bras on June 16, 1815, has been for ever rendered famous by Lord Byron. Some of us who know Geneva will remember the gorgeous monument to his eldest son Charles William Ferdinand, while the bequest of the surviving brother to his cousin, the Duke of Cumberland,* claiming still to be King of Hanover, awakens memories connected with the war of 1866, and Prince Bismarck's subsequent determined assertion of German Unity at all price.†

Probably no one in Europe more fully appreciates the military skill, combined with conspicuous bravery, shown by the Hanoverians at Langensalza in June

* Hanover was elevated into a kingdom by the Treaty of Vienna in 1814–1815, and the then Duke of Cambridge acted as British Viceroy until Ernest Duke of Cumberland, fifth son of George the Third, was made King of Hanover after the death of his brother William the Fourth. Queen Victoria was debarred from this kingdom, as the Salic law prevailed throughout Brunswick-Luneburg, so that henceforth a complete separation ensued between England and the Guelphic territories in Germany. The Duke of Cumberland's son George Frederick was known as the blind king, and lost his sovereign independence in 1866. His son Ernest Augustus, who married the Princess Thyra of Denmark, is the present Duke of Cumberland.

† These two last Dukes were children of a Baden Princess, and when Napoleon held Prussia in his grasp between 1806 and 1813, they were left in the former principality. Napoleon, however, attempted to seize their persons by stratagem, but failed.—Sir A. Halliday's 'House of Guelph,' p. 201.

1866, than the Emperor William's great Minister. The victory they won was brilliant, but on the following day King George's soldiers were overwhelmed by superior numbers, and forced to surrender.

Speaking broadly, the reigns of George the First and George the Second were rendered famous by the intellectual struggle waged for political supremacy between Walpole and Bolingbroke, much as in George the Third's time Pitt and Fox have cast a halo around the days wherein they lived. Chatham, on the other hand, shone forth resplendent without a rival near his oratorical throne, at the end of George the Second's reign and far into that of his successor. George the Fourth had a Minister in George Canning whose pictorial eloquence and happy wit has not been surpassed. The reign of William the Fourth was celebrated for the struggles of Lyndhurst and Croker against the Reform Bill, and its defence by the eloquence of Macaulay and the skilful debating of Stanley.

But it may be doubted if two greater forensic giants than Disraeli and Gladstone have ever contended for supremacy on the floor of the House of Commons. In the early part of Queen Victoria's reign Lord Melbourne, the Whig Prime Minister, guided the young Sovereign's counsels with tact and devotion, while the Tories were led by the Duke of Wellington and Sir Robert Peel. Palmerston has written his name indelibly in history by his long and successful tenure of the Premiership. Lord Aberdeen will be best remembered as the great Duke of Wellington's Foreign Minister, and in connection with the origin of the Crimean war. Lord Salisbury, the present Premier, having made his mark as an excellent orator and leader, and a first-rate Foreign Minister, has now been chosen to deal with problems calculated to tax to the utmost the powers of the greatest statesman. Divers other famous names occur to us all, but space forbids their mention here.

The reign of William the Fourth is indelibly connected with royal advocacy of the Reform Bill; and amongst many grounds for grateful admiration of Queen Victoria, not the least important will be Her Gracious Majesty's readiness to accept a far wider extension of the franchise. It is no doctrinaire opinion, that the Sovereigns of England have placed their throne on a sure basis when they have trusted the majority of their subjects. Those who have held social and political converse with the masses know what a trustworthy class the working man represents, while alas! the helpless residuum is only restless because its members are miserable, and in common with the waifs and strays of upper and middle society, become dangerous when hopeless and desperate.

The present statesmen of England have here a problem to solve which concerns national existence. The population of this country at the Peace of Utrecht in 1713 amounted to 5,000,000. At that signed in Paris during 1815 it was 15,000,000, while in 1878 the total was 33,881,966. The figures of 1888 remain to be ascertained.

Little wonder is it that men look towards the Colonies for the expansion their country needs, while a steady resolve to stand shoulder to shoulder in defence of the unity of the Empire, avoiding the mistakes made when we lost America, is perhaps the one general sentiment upon which we all agree.

But the means to such an end, and the measure of federation to be attained, are not yet whispered officially, although experts agree that the Mother Country and her Colonies should be protected by a common navy, and rely on the same hands and hearts in the hour of peril.*

That constant inquiry should be made as to the possibility of relieving the pressure of unemployed workmen in large cities and their commercial

* Mr. J. A. Froude, after examining the question through converse with the statesmen of our Australian Colonies, has arrived at the conclusion that a cordon of maritime defence may be and should be forthwith drawn around the British Empire, although he deprecates hasty efforts to secure complete Imperial Federation. Moreover he says, "We can give them back the old and glorious flag."—'Oceana,' new edition, 1886, p. 339. The same view is held by Mr. C. Kinloch Cooke, who, speaking of Australian preponderance, says: "The area of Australia is so vast, and its interests so varied, when compared to the other dependencies of Great Britain, that these interests cannot be adequately treated by a Board of Advice that includes representatives from all our colonial possessions."—'Nineteenth Century Review,' November, 1886. In the late Sir Peter Scratchley's opinion, "the several Governments should combine and establish one general scheme of naval defence to be worked in conjunction with the Imperial navy."—'Australian Defences and New Guinea,' C. Kinloch Cooke, p. 58. The English Government will have to sacrifice several prejudices if they are to remain in complete unison with their Colonial brethren, who naturally ask for such social equality before the law as circumstances allow the Mother Country to give.

suburbs, is patent to all who have dwelt in such localities and mingled with the people.*

It is not within the province of this work to encroach upon the task of contemporary chroniclers bent on recording the wonderful changes in science, art, medicine, and philanthropy, which have characterised the reign of Queen Victoria. But it is nevertheless right to join in the almost universal chorus which hails the sage Sovereign of Great Britain as a genuine defender of Religion, and an ever careful guardian of the interests of all her subjects.

The history of no time and no land records a period so glorious in progress of every kind as the fifty years of England under the rule of Queen Victoria. Though clouds hang threatening on the horizon, the past offers happy augury that they will vanish ere long before the sun of PLENTY, CONTENTMENT and PEACE.

* Lord Salisbury has said that he waits for the pressure of public opinion to arm him in dealing with this demon of over-population. Unfortunately, now that the great Prince Consort and the good Lord Shaftesbury are gone, no external agency is likely to bring sufficient influence to bear, for political it must not be.

The writer desires to record an experience of several months spent amongst these distressed ones in Battersea during the past winter when administering a fund for the relief of dire local want by means of supplying labour. Week by week would the sad procession of eager seekers for subsistence pass through the bureau of labour, 80 per cent. at least being workmen professing recognized trades. Half fed, half clothed, stunted in height, and unkempt in person, nothing saved these poor people from desperation but the desire to feed their wives and little ones. A large proportion tell us they are never sure of employment even in the height of summer, and their hopelessness bids fair to increase as time goes on.

O. V. Morgan, Esq., M.P., and John S. Gilliat, Esq., M.P., have the statistics of this attempt to touch the fringe of a great subject, and that they may bring the matter before Parliament is the fervent hope of the writer.

APPENDIX.

THE writer of this work, being Churchwarden of St. Mary's, Battersea, for the year ending Easter 1887, became aware of the fact that no inscription marked the exact spot where Lord Bolingbroke's remains rested. In the year 1878, it became necessary, for sanitary reasons, to disturb the crypt, and accordingly a faculty was obtained from the Home Office for the re-arrangement of the coffins under St. Mary's Church. The dust of the statesman who negotiated the Treaty of Utrecht was straightway placed under the crypt below the Communion-table.

Now although the archives of St. Mary's Church might have furnished data enabling some future antiquarian to localise approximately the place of Lord Bolingbroke's sepulture, yet the exact spot could only be determined by local tradition, after the eye-witnesses of the above-mentioned changes had passed away. To furnish a more trustworthy record —the present Lord Bolingbroke having given ready acquiescence, and Edward Wood, Esq., the people's Churchwarden, heartily concurring—the following inscription was placed on a raised stone tablet in the crypt, over the exact place where the eloquent Minister rests :—

Henry St. John,
VISCOUNT BOLINGBROKE,
Secretary of State
to Queen Anne.
Born 1678. Died 1751.

A visit to the old Manor-house of the Bolingbrokes, within a stone's throw of St. Mary's Church, or such part of it as has escaped destruction, discloses frescoed apartments of the style of Verrio, while the famous Cedar-Chamber, where Pope and the elder Pitt met the noble owner, is none the worse for an occasional irruption of Father Thames, who looks in when there is a very high tide. The premises are in the possession of Messrs. Dives and Mayhew, corn-merchants.

INDEX.